JOHN GREENLEAF WHITTIER

by **LEWIS LEARY**

Columbia University

 6

Twayne Publishers, Inc.   ::   New York

FOR MARTHA

Preface

WHITTIER, it seems to me, has been victimized alike by his modesty and his prolixity. I am not much of a poet, he said, and then he put together four solid volumes of collected verse to prove it. The evidence thus marshalled against him has been in a double sense overwhelming— in its bulk and in its massive testimony to the truth of his appraisal. Perhaps he should have said instead, I am not often a poet, for a reading of all that he wrote reveals among the rubble much which repays brief attention. But if not a great or always a good poet, Whittier is more than just representative of his tumultuous time and provincial place. Within the range of his competence, his notes are often pure and sometimes sustained. Certainly they have occasionally been arranged to simple melodies which are arresting and attractive. Now and then, especially during his middle years when he tried less hard, they speak of scenes or moods or aspirations which only poetry can recall.

My purpose in this brief review of his writings has not been to rediscover Whittier, for he has never really disappeared. It has been to read what he wrote, carefully and with as much discrimination as possible, and then to talk about those writings which, divorced from attachment to place or personality, seemed most interesting. The task has not been difficult; for, even when garrulous, Whittier is a pleasant man to be with. Though I have tried not to impose on him by using varieties of critical approaches which his verse was not built to withstand, I have attempted to test his writings by rigorous standards. The problem, I think, has been to discover what Whittier, who spoke so clearly to his own time, has to say to ours. I have tried throughout to speak as simply of him as he spoke of many things.

In reviewing details of Whittier's literary career I have drawn with gratitude on materials gathered by Whitman Bennett, Thomas Franklin Currier, Albert Mordell, John A.

Pollard, and especially his "official" biographer, Samuel T. Pickard; and I have, I hope, resisted temptations to speak of matters in Whittier's life which are not of public record. Why he did what he did or failed to do what he did not do seems to me of speculative concern beyond the intention of this essay. Whenever possible, I have allowed Whittier to speak for himself, respecting his proper reticences. Several of my friends will find their voices reproduced here, only partly disguised by my accent—Hyatt H. Waggoner especially, and George Arms; Jerome Hamilton Buckley, Edwin Harrison Cady, Harry Hayden Clark, Howard R. Floan, and Eleanor M. Tilton; and John B. Pickard, whom I do not know but who seems to me to understand more about Whittier as a writer than anyone else. Not least, my gratitude extends to Sylvia E. Bowman whose neat editorial huswifery has lightened my labors. Any one of them might have done this small book better than I, but none, I think, would have had more pleasure in doing it.

LEWIS LEARY

Columbia University
April 8, 1961

Contents

Chronology

1807   December 17, born on farm near Haverhill, Massachusetts, eldest son and second child of John and Abigail Hussey Whittier. Attended country schools.

1826   June 8, first poem, "The Exile's Departure," printed in the *Newburyport Free Press*, edited by William Lloyd Garrison. Beginning of lifelong friendship.

1827   May 1, entered Haverhill Academy. Poems by Whittier appeared in various newspapers. During the winter 1827-28, he taught school.

1828   November 8, first prose article (on Burns) printed in the *Haverhill Gazette*. In December, Whittier entered the printing and publishing offices in Boston of W. and W. R. Collier, where he edited the *American Manufacturer*, a pro-Clay paper.

1829   August, returned to farm; from January to June, 1830, edited the *Haverhill Gazette*.

1830   June to July, 1832, edited the *New England Weekly Review* at Hartford, Connecticut; returned to Haverhill early in 1832. Father died June 11.

1831   February, *Legends of New England* published (prose), Whittier's first book. *Moll Pitcher* published (revised, 1840). During these years Whittier's writing steadily increased in bulk, and he became known as a newspaper contributor.

1833   Published *Justice and Expediency* (Haverhill), first formal antislavery pronouncement. In November, elected delegate to the National Anti-Slavery Convention in Philadelphia.

1835   Elected to the Massachusetts Legislature. *Mogg Megone* published in the *New England Magazine* (March-April), appearing in book form in 1836. Whittier now commenced his career of agitation which exposed him and his friends to mob violence.

1836　Editor, the *Haverhill Gazette*. Sold the Haverhill farm in April; removed to Amesbury in July.

1837　*Poems written during the Progress of the Abolition Question in the United States* (Boston). Whittier active as a lobbyist and politician in New York. In October, first poem in the *Democratic Review;* Whittier contributed to it for ten years.

1838　Active in abolitionist propaganda in Philadelphia, with frequent trips to Massachusetts. Finally returned to Amesbury, which became his headquarters. *Poems* (Philadelphia).

1843　*Lays of My Home and Other Poems* (Boston).

1844　Briefly editor of the Amesbury *Village Transcript* (became the *Essex Transcript*). *Miscellaneous Poems* (Boston).

1845　Made contributing editor to the *National Era* (to 1860). *The Stranger in Lowell* (Boston).

1846　*Voices of Freedom* (Philadelphia).

1849　*Margaret Smith's Journal* appeared serially in the *National Era* and later in the year published as a book. *Poems* (Boston).

1850　London edition of *Poetical Works. Songs of Labor and Other Poems* (Boston) and *Old Portraits and Modern Sketches* (Boston).

1853　*The Chapel of the Hermits and Other Poems* (Boston).

1854　*Literary Recreations and Miscellanies* (Boston).

1855　Read "The Panorama" at Tremont Temple, Boston (book form, 1856).

1857　"Blue and Gold" edition of *Poetical Works.* "The Gift of Tritemus" in the first number of the *Atlantic Monthly.* Mother died.

1860　January 7, sister Mary died. *Home Ballads, Poems and Lyrics* (Boston).

1863 "Barbara Frietchie" in the October *Atlantic Monthly*. *In War Time and Other Poems* (Boston).

1864 September 3, sister Elizabeth died.

1865 "Laus Deo" in the *Independent*, February 9.

1866 *Snow-Bound* (Boston) published; first volume to bring Whittier considerable money. *Prose Works* (Boston, 2 vols.).

1867 *Maud Muller* published. During 1867-68 Whittier, whose health was never good, was severely ill. *National Lyrics* (Boston) and *The Tent on the Beach and Other Poems* (Boston).

1869 *Among the Hills and Other Poems* (Boston) and *Poetical Works* (Boston).

1870 *Ballads of New England* (Boston).

1871 *Miriam and Other Poems* (Boston). Whittier edited *Child Life*, a poetical anthology (Boston).

1872 *The Pennsylvania Pilgrim and Other Poems* (Boston); edited *The Journal of John Woolman* (Boston).

1874 Edited *Child Life in Prose* (Boston); published *Mabel Martin and Other Poems* (Boston). Household edition of *Works*.

1875 *Hazel Blossoms* (Boston).

1876 Edited *Songs of Three Centuries* (Boston).

1877 Seventieth birthday celebrated widely; *Atlantic Monthly* dinner. *Favorite Poems* (Boston).

1878 *The Vision of Echard and Other Poems* (Boston).

1880 W. M. Rossetti contributed critical biography to London edition of *Complete Poetical Works*.

1881 *The King's Missive and Other Poems* (Boston).

1883 *The Bay of Seven Islands and Other Poems* (Boston).

1886 *Saint Gregory's Guest and Recent Poems* (Boston).

1887 Eightieth birthday widely celebrated.

1888 *Complete Poetical and Prose Works* (Boston, 7 vols.).

1890 *At Sundown* (Boston). Whittier died on September 7.

THE MAN

> Ah! the grand old man!! A fanatic all his
> life, and yet so profoundly sincere; hating
> what he deemed crime, but ever tender
> towards the supposed criminal.
>
> —PAUL HAMILTON HAYNE

> It is easier to leave Snow-Bound and a dozen other items
>   in or out of
> The school curriculum than it is to have written them . . .
> It is so much easier to forget than to have been Mr.
>   Whittier.
> He put the names of our places into our poems and he
>   honored us with himself;
> And is for us but not altogether, because larger than us.
>
> —WINFIELD TOWNLEY SCOTT

CHAPTER 1

The Village Poet, 1807-1832

From my heart I give thee joy,—
I was once a barefoot boy!

. . . .

All too soon these feet must hide
In the prison cells of pride,
Lose the freedom of the sod,
Like a colt's for work be shod.

—"The Barefoot Boy"

JOHN GREENLEAF WHITTIER was above everything else a good man. His consistent Quaker goodness was his strength and to worldly eyes his weakness. It was goodness more simply devout than the pinched but proud New England goodness of Ralph Waldo Emerson or the equally aspiring but less well-focused goodness of Henry Wadsworth Longfellow, both of whom became his friends. Built four-square on a foundation of industry, frugality, patience, and independence, it looked beyond creed or law to promptings of the still, small voice within which spoke to him directly of truths which otherwise he might not know. It rested on assumptions of goodness in all men and on assurance that words could find ways to waken men to awareness of responsibilities to the best within them. Loving nature and loving man, but loving more the spirit of which they were emblems, Whittier wrote for more than sixty years of relations among these three. His life of quiet aspiration and strenuous humanitarian activity offers a fair opportunity for consideration of the extent to which aspiration and activity are profitable to a man of letters, and of what beyond these a poet's equipment must consist.

I *Country Life*

Whittier was born on December 17, 1807, in a farmhouse which his great-great-grandfather had built some three miles northeast of Haverhill in northern Massachusetts close to the New Hampshire line and not far from the Merrimack River. "Our old homestead," he later wrote, "nestled under a long range of hills which stretched off to the west. It was surrounded by woods in all directions save to the southeast, where a break in the leafy wall revealed a vista of low green meadows, picturesque with wooded islands and jutting capes of upland. Through these a small brook . . . wound silently and scarcely visible."

The memory of this simple countryside never left him. Whittier always remembered the "hills stretching off to the south and green meadows to the east; the small stream which comes noisily down its ravine, washing the old garden wall and softly lapping on fallen stones and mossy roots of beeches and hemlocks; the tall sentinel poplars at the gateway; the oak forest, sweeping unbroken to the northern horizon; the grass-grown carriage path, with its crude and crazy bridge." This "dear old landscape of my boyhood lives stretched before me," he said, a "picture which I have borne with me in all my wanderings."

But Whittier was not greatly a wanderer. He was to leave the Merrimack valley for Boston and Hartford, New York, Philadelphia, and Washington, but never for long. Except for Thoreau, he was the only important writer of nineteenth-century New England who was country born and bred, and who remained a country man throughout his life. Even more than Robert Frost, who later moved into and then beyond a rural environment, Whittier spoke in words which echo the essential simplicity—the lack of complication and the limitations—of his country background.

Whittier did not write invariably in praise of rural life. Like Robert Frost, he knew its hardships as well as its instructive graces. In this green and sunken pocket of inland hills men worked hard, and women also, and boys who were large enough to hold a hoe or tend the cows or follow oxen behind a plow. It was a harsh, unfertile land which took its toll in heartbreak and men. Here since 1688 four generations of Whittiers had toiled, and the land was not yet subdued to their will. The meadows were little more than bogs, wet most of the year, and the upland fields were strewn with stumps and boulders which seemed to spring maliciously from the earth. Whittier remembered "stumbling over the rough hassocks, and sinking knee deep in the black mire, raking the sharp sickle-edged grass which we used to feed out to the young cattle in mid-winter when the bitter cold gave them appetite for even such fodder." He developed "an almost Irish hatred of snakes, and these meadows were full of them"— blacksnakes, and water-snakes, "and now and then an ugly spotted adder by no means pleasant to touch with bare feet."

But there was beauty there also, so that in later life the meadows were remembered for "their redeeming points. In spring mornings the black birds and bobolinks made them musical with songs; and in the evenings great bullfrogs croaked and clamored; and on summer nights we loved to watch white wreaths of fog rising and drifting in the moonlight like troops of ghosts, with the fireflies throwing up ever and anon signals of their coming. But the brook was far more attractive, for it sheltered bathing-places, clear and white sanded, and weedy stretches where the shy pickerel loved to linger, and deep holes, where the stupid sucker stirred the black mud with his fins."[1] It was worth extra effort in cornfield or hayloft to finish the day's work in time for a late afternoon tramp through the woods with a fishing rod to Lake Kenoza, two miles away; to Brandy-brow Woods; or to Great Hill from whose crest the rolling countryside stood visible for miles in every direction—the triple peaks of Mount Monadnock to the west, Wachusetts a little to the south, the Deerfield hills ranging to the north, and to the east, not twenty miles away, the blue Atlantic stretching from Boar's Head to Cape Ann.

Whittier was a tall, slender, quiet boy who seemed alone even when he was with other people. By the time he was fifteen, he had attained his full height of just a little more than an inch under six feet; but he blushed easily, and he was more likely to listen than to speak. He preferred either to sit by himself with a book before the great fireplace in the Whittier kitchen or to watch the flame licking about oak logs as he listened to the talk of other members of the family or to tales of ghosts and goblins or local lore which some transient visitor told.

There were nine in the household of his boyhood. His father's mother, Sarah Greenleaf, had lived in the old house for almost eighty years. Her son, John Whittier, the poet's father, was a tall, sparely built, muscular man who was devout in his Quaker faith, active in local affairs, and an old-fashioned democrat who really believed, Whittier testified, in the Bill of Rights and the Declaration of Independence. A bachelor until his mid-forties, John Whittier had married Abigail Hussey in the autumn of 1804 and brought her to the family homestead where she bore him four children: Mary, born in 1806; John Greenleaf, born a year later; Matthew Franklin, five years younger than his brother; and Elizabeth Hussey, born in 1815.

Part owner of the farm was Uncle Moses, John Whittier's younger, bachelor brother. "There has always been one of that unfortunate class," his bachelor nephew later wryly recalled, "in every generation of our family." Uncle Moses was "a quiet, genial man much given to hunting and fishing; and it was one of the pleasures of our young life," related Whittier, "to accompany him on his expeditions." Many memories clustered about this favorite uncle: the building of a great barn when Whittier was thirteen, the lessons in woodcraft and angling, but principally that dreadful day when the boy was seventeen and Uncle Moses was brought into the house to die of injuries received when he had been crushed under a falling tree. Finally, as feminine counterpart to the unmarried uncle, there was Whittier's mother's maiden sister, Aunt Mercy, who lived a spinster all her adult life, faithful to the memory of a deceased young lover. An industrious helper, she was so quiet that if it had not been for her dedicated efficiency in household duties, one might have forgotten she was there.

II *Fireside Tales*

These were people whom Whittier would recall in *Snow-Bound,* years later, after all but he and his brother were gone.

He never forgot the storm-filled days of summer or winter or the dull, dark autumn days of frost and rain, when, seated about the great open fire in the farmhouse kitchen, they listened to stories of the countryside about ghosts, witches, haunted houses, and robbers—of the six little old women in short, sky-blue coats who met in witches' conclave by the banks of the brook; or of the phantom once seen bobbing for eels by the bridge. Wandering beggars, medicine men, and itinerant peddlers livened many evenings with tales of superstition or adventure.

"Twice a year, usually in the spring and autumn, we were honored with a call from Jonathan Plummer, maker of verses, peddler and poet, physician and parson—a Yankee troubadour,—first and last minstrel of the valley of the Merrimac, encircled to my wondering eyes," said Whittier, "with the very nimbus of immortality. He brought with him pins, needles, tape, and cotton-thread for my mother; jack-knives, razors, and soap for my father; and verses of his own composing, coarsely printed and illustrated with crude woodcuts, for the delectation of the younger members of the family. No love-sick youth could drown himself, no deserted maiden bewail the moon, no rogue mount the gallows without fitting memorials in Plummer's verses."[2]

Perhaps these tales and these verses set young Whittier to writing. His schoolmates in the district school remember that his rhymes flowed freely on any occasion, that his slate was filled with verses surreptitiously passed among them. His father testified that the boy had written rhymes as soon as he could write at all, but with such secrecy that only a cleaning of the attic where he hid them brought them to the family's attention. It may have been the "pawky auld carle" of a wandering Scotchman who, after eating his bread and cheese and drinking his mug of cider beside the Whittier fire, broke out with songs of "Bonny Doon," "Highland Mary," and "Auld Lang Syne," who turned the boy first to the lilting rhythms of Robert Burns. Or it may have been his schoolmaster who spent winter evenings reading to the Whittier household from books of travel and adventure, and who one memorable evening read from the Scottish poet, leaving young Whittier so entranced, he said, that "I begged him to leave the book with me, and set myself at once to the task of mastering the glossary of the Scottish dialect at its close. This was about the first poetry I ever read, with the exception of the Bible (of which I had been a close student) and it had made a lasting influence upon me. I began to make rhymes myself, and to imagine stories and adventures." In fact, "I lived a sort of dual life, and in a world of fancy, as well as in the world of plain matter-of-fact about me."[3]

Books from that time on seem to have been a staple in his daily fare. The elder Whittier's farmhouse library held little besides the Bible, *Pilgrim's Progress*, some accounts of the lives of saintly Quakers,[4] and, his son remembered in *Snow-Bound*, one nameless,

> harmless novel, mostly hid
> From younger eyes, a book forbid,
> And poetry (or good or bad),
> A single book was all we had,

and that book was a "meek, drab-skirted thing," Quaker Thomas Ellwood's rhymed life of King David. But books could be borrowed from neighbors, and soon there was a volume of Shakespeare which young Whittier brought home from a boyhood visit to Boston relatives. Other books, other poets came inevitably to his hands: Byron, Wordsworth, Coleridge, and all their American imitators. And Whittier wrote experimentally and with increasing joy like each of them.

To keep up with the world beyond his farm acres, John Whittier subscribed to the *Free Press*, edited in nearby Newburyport by young William Lloyd Garrison. The humanitarian tone of its editorials, said Whittier, "awakened deep interest in our little household." He and his sisters read also the Poet's Corner; and Mary, thinking that the verses her brother made were quite as good as any she found there, secretly sent off one of his poems. Garrison, only two years older than Whittier, but greatly more experienced, tells of receiving it: "Going upstairs to my office one day, I observed a letter lying near the door . . . which on opening I found to contain an original piece of poetry for my paper. . . . The ink was pale, the handwriting very small; and, having a horror of newspaper 'original poetry' . . . my first impulse was to tear it to pieces without reading it." But he did read, and "was equally surprised and gratified to find it above mediocrity, and so gave it a place in my journal."[5]

"The Exile's Departure" appeared, therefore, in the Newburyport *Free Press* on June 8, 1826, signed "W." It was imitative and derivative, a lonely man's Byronic farewell to "scenes which delighted my youthful existence" as "shores of Hibernia recede from my view." Whittier was not only surprised but pleased also to see it in print—and he must have liked especially the editorial comment which accompanied it: "If 'W' at Haverhill will continue to favor us with pieces, beautiful as the one inserted in our editorial department today," Garrison had written, "we shall esteem it a great favor." So Whittier himself submitted a second poem, done in blank verse, called "The Deity," which told simply of an ancient prophet who discovered God, not in din of storm or earthquake, but in the still, small voice within his own heart. It bore the mark of true genius, thought Garrison. It was expert enough in phrasing to rank its author "among the bards of his country."[6]

By questioning the post-rider who had delivered the manuscript, the young editor then discovered the identity of his new contributor. "Jumping into a vehicle, I lost no time," he said, "in driving to see the youthful rustic bard." Whittier was at work in the fields, repairing fences, when Garrison arrived. Summoned to meet the literary guest, he came into the room with shrinking diffidence, almost unable to speak, blushing like a maiden. "Giving him some words of encouragement," said Garrison, "I addressed myself particularly to his parents, and urged them with great earnestness to grant him every facility for the development of his remarkable genius." He spoke of the necessity for schooling; but the nearest academy was in Newburyport, almost fifteen miles away. He warned of the mistake they would make in warring against nature if they tried to quench these "first kindlings of a flame which might burn like a star in our literary horizon." The elder Whittiers were sympathetic, but they remembered the mortgage which bound them all to labor. Garrison's most fervent pleadings succumbed finally to their kindly resistance. "Sir," said the poet's father with forthright New England practicality, "poetry will not give him bread."[7]

John Whittier was right, for forty tight-pinched years would pass before his son would find verse-making a profitable profession. The father's attitude was characteristic and not unkindly. Young Longfellow, recently graduated from Bowdoin College in Maine, had received from his sensible father the same shrewd admonition; and, since then, how many more literary young men have not been affectionately reminded that poetry will not pay? But young poets are not likely to listen to parents. All during that summer, every week until mid-September, and irregularly through the fall, Whittier submitted poems to the *Free Press*. None were really good, and Whittier was later embarrassed to remember them. They were apprentice work of a young man who stretched his talent over moods and subjects worn smooth by better poets. Byron, not Burns, seemed now his master; and Thomas Moore and Thomas Hood, and the hundreds of imitators who wrote with less skill but more sentiment. Whittier spoke ominously of "The Voice of Time," tearfully of "The Shipwreck" or "The Burial of Princess Charlotte," and with pious sincerity of "Benevolence" and the Quaker virtues of "William Penn." He wrote in lilting measure of scenes of his childhood, the familiar moss-covered banks of his own native river, the "home of my fathers—fair Merrimac's vale." In sentimental moral legend, in lines of aspiration toward simple virtues, and in affectionate description of his New England countryside, Whittier was discovering subjects which would always charm him most.

When Garrison left Newburyport a year later for larger opportunities in Boston, Whittier began to offer his verses to the *Gazette* in Haverhill, which was edited by Abijah Thayer, a good-hearted man of humanitarian interests who became a second father to the young poet. During 1827 more than fifty poems by Whittier appeared in the *Gazette*, a few unashamedly over his name; but most of them were signed "Adrian" or, when in Scotch dialect, "Donald"; or sometimes as by "Peter" or simply "W." Ambition was now seriously aroused. Whittier learned shoemaking, a profitable second, winter-time vocation among many farm people of the Merrimack valley; and he saved enough from his tiny profits to allow him late in April, 1827, to enroll at nineteen as a high school freshman at the newly organized Haverhill Academy.

Whittier was a special kind of freshman; he had a growing reputation as a village poet. "Possessing no other advantages of education than are afforded in the common town schools," yet, wrote Abijah Thayer, "we surely have reason to expect much from him." For the opening exercises of the new academy, its talented new student—described as tall, good-looking enough to be a favorite among the young ladies, but serious, ambitious, and engagingly shy—provided an original ode, which began:

Hail, Star of Science! come forth in thy splendor
  Illumine these walls—let them evermore be
A shrine, where thy vot'ries their offerings may tender
  Hallow'd by genius and sacred to thee.

Through all his life Whittier could turn off verse of this kind, foot by foot, almost at will. Enough like other verse to be recognized as properly related, it did what most people thought poetry should do—articulate their thoughts, underline their emotions, even vicariously expand their experience. If it dwelt on a plateau just above ordinary language and never soared out of sight or plunged to depths beyond common vision, it never eluded understanding and it seldom failed to elicit responsive applause. It was attractive because familiar words were set to appealing and familiar rhythms in celebration of events or emotions remembered by his country neighbors. Local fame came so quickly that the young poet had difficulty discovering that he was not writing well.

While attending school in the village, Whittier lived with the Thayers, helping as he could about the *Gazette* office, gathering materials for a history of Haverhill, and adding to his scant store of cash by after-hours bookkeeping for a local merchant. At the end of one term his funds ran out; and he became a teacher in a country school, qualifying himself for the position by the excellence of his handwriting. For one so shy the experience could not have been happy.

"The troubles of a pedagogue," he wrote in a rhymed letter to Thayer, "Nae mair my wanderin' muse shall clog." In the spring of 1828 Whittier was happy to return for another session at the academy.

His verses, more than forty of them, continued to appear in the *Gazette*. Others were placed, probably with Garrison's assistance, in Boston papers. Two even found space in the influential, literary *New England Weekly Review*, which George D. Prentice edited in Hartford. What was better, some were reprinted with pleasant words of approval in periodicals like the *Boston Spectator and Ladies Album* and the *Saturday Evening Post* in Philadelphia. When someone said of Whittier that "he borrows too largely from other poets," Thayer came stoutly to his defense: "Such richness and sublimity of language, such brilliance of imagination and delicacy of sentiment, have not, we believe, distinguished any of the early productions of the most celebrated modern poets."[8]

Praise like this could turn a young man's head. Editor Thayer was perhaps too kind. Earlier in the year he had announced in the *Gazette* that *The Poems of Adrian*, some of which had been "copied into the most respectable papers, in various sections of the Union, with strong approbation," would be published in a volume when a sufficient number of subscribers had been secured. "It is believed by his friends," wrote Thayer, "that these poems indicate genius of a high order, which deserves all possible culture. The design of thus offering his juvenile writings to the public is to raise money to assist him in obtaining a classical education."[9] Nothing came of this generous attempt to help a talented and favorite villager write his way through college. Subscribers were not forthcoming, and the volume never appeared. Further education was indefinitely postponed.

III *Journalism and Politics*

When later in 1828 Garrison arranged in Boston for Whittier to be his successor as editor of the *National Philanthropist*, a prohibitionist paper, Whittier informed Thayer that he had given up all idea of college, "for the good reason that I have no disposition to humble myself to meanness for an education—crowding myself through college upon the charities of others, and leaving it with a debt or obligation to weigh down the spirit like an incubus, and paralyze every exertion." Even his "miserable knack of rhyming," he said, would avail him nothing but struggle with debt and an inevitable return "to my original insignificance." Work on a paper like the *Philanthropist* which was dedicated to reform seemed to him not only more dignified and respectable, but "peculiarly pleasant to one who takes so deep an interest, as I really do, in the cause it is laboring to promote." He would rather be remembered as a friend to mankind than enjoy "the undying fame of a Byron."[10]

Arriving in Boston late in December, he was disappointed to discover that he would not be editor of the *National Philanthropist* for which he thought himself particularly well qualified because of his severe personal disapproval of alcoholic beverages. Instead, he was assigned at a salary of $9 a week to the *American Manufacturer,* a commercial weekly dedicated to upholding the new protective tariff, encouraging native industries, and advancing the Whig political principles of Henry Clay. Whittier's chief duty seems to have been the writing of editorials, many of them doggedly but not learnedly political, some inevitably literary. The best comprised a series addressed to the young workingmen of Boston. His cheeks like theirs, he said, had burned and his pulse had quickened with anger, when exposed to the undisguised contempt of the wealthy and arrogant. His own experience taught him that young men of their kind were deprived of advancement, "not from any defect in their moral character, their minds, or their persons, but simply because they depended upon their own exertions for their means of existence, and upon their own industry and talents for passport to public favor." Whittier's verses, appearing in almost every issue, dealt more often now with the weaknesses or duties of men than with quiet beauties of nature or romance.

During his six months in Boston, the country boy who was for the first time in a large city kept busy at his desk or in exciting talk with other literary aspirants, but not so busy that on his frequent visits to the library at the Boston Athenaeum, made necessary by the requirement of weekly prose contributions, he could not be lured from study by admiration of attractive female readers gathered there. "I always did love a pretty girl." he wrote. "Heaven grant there is no harm in it."[11] He never lost his young man's fancy, but he never lost himself in pursuit of it.

Such urban experience came to an end in the summer of 1829 when he was called home by the illness of his father. From that time until after John Whittier's death almost a year later, farm duties and family cares occupied the poet's time. Writing became a luxury, reserved for idle hours. For a few months during the winter and early spring he filled in for Thayer in managing the *Gazette* in Haverhill, doing most of the work at home, perhaps walking to town once or twice a week to put things in order for the little paper's weekly appearance. He sent occasional poetry and political essays to other journals, notably to Prentice's *New England Weekly Review*.

"Mr. Whittier," wrote Nathaniel Parker Willis in the *American Monthly Magazine* for August, "has retired to his 'farm.' He is happier than any poor-devil-Editor of us all. His crop will not be criticized. He may grow cabbages or turnips as he pleases, and his investments in mother Earth, unlike those of some of her children, will come to light again. It will not cost him much, either, to entertain his extravagant friends, the Muses. . . . We fear, however, that Quaker though he be, the country will be too quiet for him after his busy editorship."

Willis's forecast was correct. When in July, 1830, George D. Prentice was appointed to write a campaign biography of Henry Clay, Whittier was invited to replace him at Hartford as editor of the *Weekly Review*. Prentice introduced him to his readers as a gentleman of "powerful energies and . . . exalted purity and sweetness of character." For almost eighteen months then, until January, 1832, young Whittier lived in the Connecticut town, turning out an enormous stream of verse and prose—editorials, sketches, book reviews, enough to fill a good-sized volume. Freed of farm responsibilities and the necessity of hack work such as he had done in Boston, he was at twenty-four finally a full-fledged writer who moved freely among the literary circles of America's most proudly literary town. Lydia Sigourney, admired nationally as "the sweet singer of Hartford," greeted him as a friend and equal.

Whittier provided a long appreciative introduction to the *Literary Remains* of the recently deceased young local poet, John G. C. Brainard, in which he made important statements about the responsibility of native poets to use native themes. He sent poems of his own to other periodicals, as far west as Cincinnati, as far south as Philadelphia. Matters concerned with settling his father's estate made trips to Haverhill necessary; matters of politics took him to New York. Then in February, 1831, he put together his own first published book, a collection in verse and prose which he called *Legends of New England*. It was a bad book, commonplace in language; and Whittier knew it—if not then, soon. Not many years afterwards he is reported to have offered five dollars for any copy brought to him so that he could burn it.

The young man was working too hard. He was attempting too many things, burdened with too much responsibility. As he rubbed shoulders with the world and discovered evils within it which tempted men to do what they should not do and leave undone the thousand better things to which enlightened men might aspire, the weight of his new knowledge bore heavily on him. In the fall of 1831, a nervous breakdown sent him home to Haverhill in the care of a physician. After rest of several weeks, under the affectionate care of his mother and his sister Elizabeth, he returned to Hartford; but the miscellaneous activities of an editor were clearly too much for him. He was plagued with blue devils of melancholy and despair. Headaches which had bothered him from boyhood came with increasing frequency and intensity. So he gave up his fine position on the *Weekly Review* and returned early in 1832 to Haverhill in the depths of depression. "I have scarcely done anything this winter," he confessed. "There have been few days in which I have been able to write with any degree of comfort."[12]

He worked over a long poem called *Moll Pitcher* which would be published in the spring. But poetry of the kind he wrote seemed ineffectual to him. He puttered over a novel, but nothing came of that. The more he read and the more he knew of the world and its shortcomings, the more certain he was of his own inadequacies: "I love poetry with a love as warm, as fervent, as sincere, as any of the more gifted worshippers at the temple of the Muses. I consider its gift as something holy and above the fashion of the world." But he doubted now that this wondrous gift had been given him. Without it, he would have to turn aside to other routes toward distinction and profit: "Politics is the only field now open to me, and there is something inconsistent in the character of a poet and a modern politician."[13]

How much of this attitude resulted from Whittier's physical disability and its accompanying despair and how much represented clear-sighted recognition of literary shortcomings cannot be known. It has sometimes been supposed that, if he had enjoyed better health, he might have been extraordinarily successful as a newspaperman or in public service. As it was, he kept his hand in politics for the rest of his life, particularly in local Essex County politics, as an advisor and successful political manipulator. Now, in the spring of 1832, he was invited to run for Congress; but he had to refuse—or, as some would have it, was able to refuse—because he was below the required age of twenty-five. He worked with quiet diligence in support of Henry Clay against Andrew Jackson for the presidency. From his home near Haverhill he wrote with increasing earnestness about the necessity for political and moral reform. The example of his friend Garrison, who for a year had struggled courageously in Boston in the face of hostile public opinion and threat of physical violence to publish his militant abolitionist weekly, the *Liberator,* stirred Whittier's Quaker conscience: "I have done with poetry and literature," he said.[14]

After quiet months at the family farm, he could report: "My health is vastly improved; the blues have left me; I go on husking frolics, and all that sort of thing. I have put a veto on poetry; read all I can find . . . and am happy—at least, I believe I am."[15] Away from "the din and bustle of the village, with a long range of green hills stretching away to the river," he was as comfortable, he said, "as one can be, always excepting ill health." But even there, the call of events came to him. "I have found my political reputation," he said, "is more influential than my poetical; so I try to make myself a man of the world."[16] While managing the farm, he continued to send occasional contributions to political papers, as he looked from his Massachusetts hills toward a larger world where men were not always good to each other.

CHAPTER 2

Bard of Freedom, 1832-1840

And one there was, a dreamer born,
Who, with a mission to fulfil,
Had left the Muse's haunts to turn
The crank of an opinion mill,
Making his rustic reed of song
A weapon in the war with wrong.
—"The Tent on the Beach"

THE END of the year 1832 marks the beginning of a second stage in Whittier's life and work. It is also a good date to remember for other reasons. A literary era came to an end with the death in the United States of Philip Freneau, the poet of the American Revolution, and with the death abroad of Walter Scott in Scotland and Goethe in Germany. The romantic period in England came to an end. Washington Irving returned to New York after more than a decade of extraordinary success in the Old World. Emerson, recently a widower and troubled about what to make of his life, had resigned his Boston pastorate and gone abroad to seek spiritual refreshment. Poe and Hawthorne were beginning to break regularly into print. In England, Mrs. Trollope wrote disdainfully of *Domestic Manners of the Americans*. In France, de Tocqueville, returned from a visit to the United States, worked over his notes in preparation for *La Démocratie en Amérique*, his better book. The young nation was expanding and coalescing. Established literary voices, like those of Irving and Cooper, tried patiently to fit the new into established forms; Bryant visited Illinois and wrote, as an Englishman might write, of "The Prairies." Fresh voices were rising or preparing to rise. Walt Whitman was a boy of thirteen on Long Island; Thoreau was a schoolboy in Concord. Abraham Lincoln, ten years older than Whitman, was a militiaman in the Black Hawk War.

I *The Rich Materials*

Whittier, a captive restless on the family farm, was at loose ends. His father's death left debts and family responsibilities. The rugged acres of ancestral farmland required more strength and physical endurance than the poet could ever contribute. A living had to be made not only for himself but for his mother, his sister and his Aunt Mercy. Verses, even turned out with facile regularity, would not keep the larder filled; but writing was something which Whittier could do well and, given health and proper connections, do successfully. His experience in Boston and Hartford had proved that he could turn an effective phrase; and he had ideas, particularly about what people did wrong: ruining themselves with strong drink; refusing opportunities to young men handicapped by birth or by education; looking down on them because they worked with their hands; or considering them little more than slaves condemned to economic bondage. He recalled some of the things which Thomas Jefferson had said about natural rights, but even more clearly how Edmund Burke had said many of the same things with saner qualifications. For Whittier was politically no Democrat, certainly not of the Andrew Jackson variety who aroused men by appealing to their base, acquisitive natures. But near the core of Whittier's thinking was an abiding faith in democracy; and his allegiance was built on deeply rooted, personal, religious convictions.

He found himself, like many young men in any generation, confused by a world which needed correction. The nation, stirring with activity, had gotten ahead of itself. It needed reminders, he thought, that simple truths must not be forgotten. Whittier was drawn toward humanitarian philanthropy, not only by the example of his friend Garrison, but also by his Quaker assurance that all men were really equal in the eyes of God and that all men might be taught to listen to the compelling voice of God within them. He liked to recall the Puritan liberalism of John Milton, a poet infinitely greater than Whittier ever dreamed he might become, who put aside the making of verses to apply his genius to the greater task of molding contemporary thought. Whittier had discovered that his own best talent was for quiet persuasion. It must not lie useless while there was so much to correct—and when it might solve the problem of how to provide for himself and his dependents.

At twenty-five Whittier enjoyed something more than local reputation as, in the words of one of his contemporaries, "a singularly chaste and powerful writer."[1] The *Legends of New England* affirmed his early conviction that his native land was rich in lore ready to be made into literature. "It has often been said," he wrote in his introduction to Brainard's *Literary Remains*, "that the New World is deficient in the elements of poetry and romance; that its bards must of necessity linger over the classic ruins of other lands; and draw their sketches of character from foreign sources, and paint Nature under the soft beauty of an Eastern sky." But this was not true, for the New England he knew was filled with romance: "The great forest which our fathers penetrated, the red men, their struggle and their disappearance, the powwow and the war dance, the savage inroad and the English sally, the tale of superstition and scenes of witch-craft,—all these are rich materials of poetry." He admitted that we "have, indeed, no classic vale of Tempe, no haunted Parnassus, no temple gray with years, and hallowed by the generous pageantry of idol worship, no towers and castles over whose moonlit ruins gather the green pall of ivy; but we have mountains bright and beautiful as those of Greece and Italy, and forests richer and nobler than those which of old were haunted by sylph and dryad."[2]

Emerson was to echo thoughts like these only a few years later, and Whitman was to speak them with plainer intensity more than twenty years after Whittier spoke. Irving and Cooper and Bryant had already turned to native themes and scenes; and Hawthorne, three years older than Whittier, was beginning to find opportunities for profound moral insights within the framework of local history. Like Irving, however, Whittier retold or embellished tales now mainly for the sake of story—the heartbreak or adventure which the narrative revealed. The prose and verse in the *Legends of New England* was set forth in smoothly sentimental, conventional language which, mounting sometimes to rhetorical extravagance or melodrama, seldom pierced beneath the tale toward insights suggestive of meaning.

Literature was literature; life was life; and there was a gap between them that the young poet did not bridge. Whittier at this period has been correctly described as a fanciful romanticist, an apostle of Scott-like localism who was interested in the lurid, the strange, the sentimental, and the dreamy. "The Weird Gathering" was a story which Cotton Mather had told of a congress of witches and prestidigious spirits gathered at Salem, and Whittier retold it plainly, as Irving might, without exercise of imagination of the kind which makes Hawthorne's essentially similar "Young Goodman Brown" infinitely the better story. "The Murdered Lady" recounts a sad and sentimental tale of pirate days in old Marblehead. "The Spectre Warriors" retells a Gloucester legend of Indian warfare.

"I have attempted," Whittier said in his preface to the collection, "to present in interesting form some of the popular traditions and legends of New England. The field is a new one—and I have but partially explored it. New England is rich in traditionary lore. A thousand associations of superstition and manly daring and romantic adventure, are connected with her green hills and her pleasant rivers." He would do what Brainard had done, only better and more consistently, and what Irving had done so spectacularly well for another region. Having plunged, he said, "into the dusky receptacle of ghost stories and Indian traditions . . . with good luck we shall make something of them—old and ragged as they are. . . . If nothing else is gained, we shall, at least, have the satisfaction of ministering to our natural vanity:

" 'Tis pleasant sure to see one's name in print—
"A book's a book, although there's nothing in't."[3]

Though one critic thought the *Legends of New England* "the most agreeable work of its kind since *The Sketch Book*," others have thought it "juvenile and extravagantly rhetorical."[4] Whittier's prose was not so smoothly good as Irving's, nor was his verse as ruminatively serene as Bryant's. But he had learned from them, and from Scott and Wordsworth also, that literature might derive from common things. He learned from Coleridge, but mostly from Milton, that it might also bend to serve a common good. What he had not learned, and perhaps never mastered securely, was that writing dedicated to moral uplift requires something besides if it is to be cherished also as literature.

While he remained at home, through dreary months of soul-searching and hesitation, managing the farm, occasionally hitching a team for the drive overland to the mouth of the Merrimack, where apples and vegetables might be exchanged for salt fish brought in from the sea, Whittier continued doggedly to write. In the spring of 1832 he published in Boston a twenty-eight page poem called *Moll Pitcher*, the "offspring," he admitted in a Preface, "of a few weeks of such leisure as is afforded by my indisposition," and "given to the world in all its original negligence." The poem tells, not of the celebrated heroine of the American Revolution, but of a witch who casts a spell over a fair young maiden who then goes mad with grief because she believes her sailor lover has been lost at sea. But he is not lost, and his faithful attentions bring back the maiden's sanity as "the thousand fancies which were nursed in madness Vanish one by one." They live happily, and their fair daughter ministers with gentle care at the deathbed of the evil witch who had threatened their happiness. *Moll Pitcher* was not well done, nor did it do well. Whittier was later ashamed, he said, to acknowledge it as his own.[5]

And he worked now over another and longer poem, *Mogg Megone*, based on a half-true and half-imagined Indian legend, but it was not to be completed nor published until 1835. Mogg was a wily Indian sachem in league with a treacherous renegade white man who had a beautiful daughter whom the Indian desired. In exchange for a tract of forest land the white father gave his daughter to the red man, who, as part of the pre-nuptial bargain, murdered the white adventurer who had formerly seduced the girl. Indian-like, Mogg fell prey to the white man's firewater; and, while in drunken slumber, he was murdered by his new white bride, because she could not forget her former lover whom the Indian had slain. Escaping to a Jesuit mission in Maine, she confessed her sins; but she was killed when English rangers attacked the settlement and brutally massacred all its inhabitants. Why Whittier was attracted to so grisly a tale cannot be known. He was afterwards to refer to Mogg as "that 'big injun' strutting round in Walter Scott's plaids," and to object to the poem on both moral and aesthetic grounds: it was not in good taste; neither was it, he said, "calculated to do good." "I had no business to make him," an older Whittier said of Mogg, "and it is poetical justice that he should haunt me like another Frankenstein."[6] Other people, however, liked it better than he; and it became one among his early poems which was often reprinted.

II *Crusade for Liberation*

Justice was becoming a word with increasingly important meanings to Whittier. Garrison's activities as editor of the *Liberator* seemed a constant rebuke to him—he who sat at home rattling verses which had no meaning beyond themselves. He recognized his own as like other poetry produced in the United States, which he had described three years earlier in the *American Manufacturer* as lacking "character of thought" and that "deep, engrossing interest" which could "chain down our sympathies and work upon sterner passions." It was "the tinsel and drapery of poetry, without the substance."[7]

So he pledged himself, he said, to "the reforming spirit, which is abroad in our land."[8] He had already written temperance poems and had editorialized on the demon rum and the evils of imprisonment for debt; and these remained among the causes he was to champion for the rest of his life: women should have greater rights; workmen should have shorter hours; churchmen should remember more often the gospel of love; and justice should be done to the American Indian. But the most compelling to him of all reforms, from this time onward, was that which looked toward the abolition of slavery. Among his first writings as an independent editor three years before had been warnings that the sword of vengeance would surely smite his countrymen unless they rid themselves of the sin of human bondage. Garrison's example, his own convictions, and his need to find a place for himself combined to drive him toward forthright commitment of his talent.

Whittier was nominated in 1833 as a delegate from Haverhill to the convention of the Massachusetts Society for the Suppression of Intemperance. Although he believed that men should take better care and make wiser use of powers with which God had endowed them, not blurring them with alcohol, Whittier was convinced that man's injustice to other men was more criminal by far than what man did to himself. The terrible stain of Negro slavery spread hideously over his land, making mockery of every ideal of human freedom to which its people gave lip-service. When Garrison challenged him in the spring of 1833 with "Whittier enlist!— your talents, zeal, influence—all are needed,"[9] he responded, therefore, without hesitation. He who had known few Negroes of any kind, and who had probably by 1833 seldom seen a slave, became an ardent recruit in Garrison's crusade for liberation.

It was like the Macedonian cry to Paul, this plea for human justice. "Shamed be the hands that idly fold" in times like these, said Whittier in "The Summons." Whatever the charms of village life, of nature and old legends, and of idle song, these must be put aside for more dedicated occupation. Whittier resolved to "fight the battles of the Lord" with every talent which he had. And so, as he explained in "The Panorama," he left

> the green and pleasant paths of song,
> The mild, sweet words which soften and adorn,
> For sharp rebuke and bitter laugh of scorn.

From 1833, when he was twenty-five, until the end of the Civil War more than thirty years later, Whittier dedicated his most active endeavors to abolition. His health broke down more than once under the strain and his Quaker upbringing made him refuse to condone physical conflict; and, as war approached, he withdrew more and more from active participation. He traded his popularity as a poet for the contribution which his skill with words could make in convincing his countrymen of the corroding evil of slavery. Persuading many, angering many, he became a controversial figure, a symbol of dedicated, pious partisanship: "For twenty years," he said, "my name would have injured the circulation of any of the literary or political journals of the country."[10] The wonder is that, toward the end of this extended period of propaganda, a poet emerged who was to speak more surely and simply within the range to which his experience limited him than any American poet had spoken before or than any but a few have spoken since.

His first onslaught was in prose. With the publication of *Justice and Expediency* in June, 1833, Whittier projected himself at once to the center of controversy. Written with blunt directness, this pamphlet set forward its argument in language so plain that no one could misunderstand it. Like Thomas Paine's *Common Sense* more than half a century before, it spoke what many men had thought, thus providing a rallying ground on which men of humanitarian good will could meet and recognize one another. No half-way measures in combating the evils of slavery would do, neither the colonization of free Negroes in Africa nor the boycotting of slave-grown produce. Only immediate emancipation, beginning at once with the District of Columbia and the territories under direct federal control, could cleanse the United States from the dreadful stain which certified her guilt before the world.

Yet the abolitionists for whom Whittier spoke advocated no use of physical force, nor was Whittier himself, as some modern admirers would claim him, a militant man.[11] Of his kind of abolitionist, he said: "They seek to obtain their object, not with the weapons of violence, but with those of reason and truth, prayer to God, and entreaty to man." They sought to impress on every heart true doctrines of the rights of all men and to establish, they hoped for all time, the incontrovertible and fundamental truth of human liberty which states that no man can hold his brother in bondage. They believed that, this truth about man's right to freedom admitted, slavery as an institution must inevitably fall, for no human law or custom could controvert the word of God. To them, it was only necessary that the heart and conscience be touched; then all men would respond. This doctrine of human rights must therefore be shouted above the housetops, whispered in chimney corners, poured forth from pulpit and press, and seared deep into the consciousness of every American to form an irreducible first premise, a cornerstone on which public conscience might be constructed. Ours has always been a government of opinion, Whittier explained: "change the current of public opinion, and slavery will be swept away."

Sometimes, as thus in *Justice and Expediency*, Whittier remained, therefore, patiently explanatory. Slavery was a relic of outworn times; old-fashioned and wasteful, it exerted a pernicious influence on the nation's economy as well as an evil influence on men. But he was most persuasive when his rhetoric ran a little wild, when he raised his voice and gestured for accent like a revivalist at the pitch of persuasive passion. He wanted neither the violence of war nor the bitterness of sectional prejudice but only peace; he exhorted, "the peace of universal love, of catholic sympathy, the peace of common interest, a common feeling, a common humanity." As long as slavery was tolerated, he was sure that no such peace could exist, for "liberty and slavery cannot dwell in harmony together."

Slaveholders were not free men; slaveholding states were really neither free nor prosperous. How baneful, said Whittier, were the effects of man's injustice: "We are told of grass-grown streets, of crumbling mansions, of beggared planters and barren plantations, of fear from without, of terror within." Fields once fertile were wasted and tenantless because the curse of slavery had poisoned the earth. A moral mildew had settled over the land, "as if the finger of the everlasting God had written on the soil of the slave-holder the language of his displeasure."

To find such phrases hollow, meaningless or even untrue, is not to underestimate them as effective weapons of persuasion nor to doubt the sincerity with which they were written, even when they rise shrilly to intimations of terror. Repent, Whittier would say, before it is too late. Set free these dusky brothers before they look into their own hearts and listen to the voice within them which tells them that they are free. On discovering his God-given gift of freedom and discovering also his superiority in strength over his debilitated white master, the Negro would then rise in righteous insurrection, his torch at every doorway, his knife at every throat. "Where then will be the pride, the beauty and the chivalry of the South? The smoke of her torment will rise upward like a thick cloud visible over the whole earth." A day must come when men will rise in revolt. Revolution "hangs above us, reddening with the elements of destruction."[12]

The appeal to sense and the rhetorical fervor of *Justice and Expediency* spread Whittier's fame at once through the land. An edition of five hundred copies which he paid for and distributed himself was soon exhausted. Lewis Tappan, an open-handed philanthropist in New York, saw to its reprinting in the *Anti-Slavery Reporter* in September, 1833, in an initial issue of five thousand copies, and then probably many thousands more. Moses Brown, a wealthy Quaker in Rhode Island, had it copied into the *Providence Journal.* The pamphlet set men talking, made them think. Sober men responded to its judicious sobriety, warm-hearted men to the sincerity of its benevolence, and hot-headed men used it as a spur to action. It upset charitable men who professed love toward their black brothers but never bothered to do much about them.

Not all response was favorable. Whittier was attacked by proslavery editors and politicians of North and South as a radical, misty-eyed and impractical. To them such passionate declarations as his could upset delicate political balances. Trade would be harmed, the whole national economy thrown out of balance. It even seemed unpatriotic to point thus directly at shortcomings among his countrymen. What would the world think? If everyone talked as Whittier talked, there would be trouble indeed. Yet, it was answered, if people did not speak out as he had spoken, the freedoms of which his countrymen boasted would continue to be mockery.

During the summer of 1834 Whittier composed a "Hymn Written for the Meeting of the Anti-Slavery Society, at

Chatham Street Chapel, New York," in which he looked forward to the time when "every land and tongue and clime" would have heard the divine message of the necessity for human love,

> When, smitten as with fire from Heaven,
> The captive's chain shall sink in dust;
> And to his fettered soul be given
> The glorious freedom of the just.

Soon he was more actively engaged. In December, 1833, he had joined Garrison and other New England abolitionists as a delegate to the National Anti-Slavery Convention in Philadelphia. In spite of his youth, he became one of the secretaries of the convention and a member of the committee which, under Garrison's chairmanship, drew up the Declaration of Sentiments which would define and govern abolitionist activity for many years. He was prouder, he later said, of his part in the composition of this document, than of anything he had ever written or was to write.

Meanwhile, Whittier contributed to the *Liberator,* the *New England Magazine* in Boston, and the *Gazette* in Haverhill. He wrote of "Toussaint L'Ouverture," the brave black chieftain in Haiti who suffered treachery at the hands of Napoleon and his colonial governors. He wrote of "The Slave Ships," the loathsome prisons in whose dark holds men, women, and little children were chained amid indescribable filth; where disease wrought awful havoc; and from which the dead and dying were tossed in terror overboard by white crewmen. Every stop was pulled wide which might sound forth to catch the ear or to fill the eye of Whittier's benevolent countrymen. Stripped of subtleties of mood or sentiment, his verse rang with strident, anger-choked, or tear-choked pleas for justice and freedom for all men.

Most effective of his early abolitionist verses were the stanzas entitled "Expostulation," beginning "Our fellow-countrymen in chains," which, published in the *Liberator* on September 13, 1834, were reprinted in antislavery papers all over the country. They were also circulated widely in a broadside, half of which was taken up with a woodcut of a Negro, shackled hand and foot, who, kneeling in supplication, asked: "Am I not a man and a brother?" Nothing which Whittier wrote expressed more passionately his hatred of the "damning shade of Slavery's curse" which shadowed the reputation of his country in the eyes of the world:

> Just God! and shall we calmly rest,
> The Christian's scorn—the heathen's mirth—
> Content to live the lingering jest
> And by-word of a mocking earth?
> Shall our own glorious land retain
> That curse which Europe scorns to bear?
> Shall our own brethren drag the chain
> Which not even Russia's menials wear?

In 1835 Whittier was elected to the Massachusetts legislature where, though not active in debate, he played an influential part as a skillful manipulator who worked behind the scenes to further such measures of reform as abolition of capital punishment. While attending a session of the legislature in October, 1835, he watched a Boston mob, led by men of property and standing, storm into an antislavery meeting at which Garrison was speaking and drag him through the streets toward jail with a rope around his neck. Because abolitionists were troublemaking people, mobs rose often to oppose them; and Whittier himself faced crowds of angry countrymen more than once. That summer in Concord, New Hampshire, where he appeared at an antislavery rally, he was pelted with rotten eggs and mud and stones. Even quiet Haverhill was not without its incident of assault against proponents of abolition. Stones were thrown, windows were broken; a loaded cannon was dragged to the door of the meetinghouse to frighten the dangerously dedicated people within. "America," said Whittier, "is working everlasting disgrace for her future name."

When proslavery citizens of Boston, meeting at Faneuil Hall on August 21, 1835, proposed to silence the abolitionists by demanding suppression of the right to free speech, lest it

endanger the economic structure on which Yankee commercial
enterprise was built, Whittier in "Stanzas for the Times"
asked scornfully:

> Is this the land our fathers loved,
>   The freedom which they toiled to win?
> Is this the soil whereon they moved?
>   Are these the graves they slumber in?
> Are we the sons by whom are borne
> The mantles which the dead have worn?
>
> .   .   .   .
>
> Shall tongues be mute, when deeds are wrought
>   Which well might shame extremest hell?
> Shall freemen lock the indignant thought?
>   Shall Pity's bosom cease to swell?
> Shall Honor bleed?—shall Truth succumb?
> Shall pen, and press, and soul be dumb?
>
> .   .   .   .
>
> No; guided by our country's laws,
>   For truth, and right, and suffering man
> Be ours to strive in Freedom's cause,
>   As Christian's may, as freemen can!
> Still pouring on unwilling ears
> That truth oppression only fears.

When it was reported from South Carolina in the Charleston
Courier in September of 1835 that the clergymen of that
city had in a body attended a proslavery meeting, "adding
by their presence to the impressive character of the scene,"
Whittier exploded in indignation against "Clerical Oppressors":

> Just God! and these are they
> Who minister at thy altar, God of Right!
> Men who their hands with prayer and blessing lay
>   On Israel's Ark of light!
>
> What! preach, and kidnap men?
> Give thanks, and rob thy own afflicted poor?
> Talk of thy glorious liberty, and then
>   Bolt hard the captive's door?

"Proud hypocrites," he called them, "whose hire is from the price of blood," who from tasseled pulpits pervert and distort the voice of God.

> How long, O Lord! how long
> Shall such a priesthood barter truth away
> And in Thy name, for robbery and wrong
> At Thy own altars pray?

When in 1836 Calhoun introduced to the Congress a bill which would make it a penal offense for postmasters in any state, district, or territory "knowingly to deliver to any person whatever, any pamphlet, handbill, or other printed paper or pictorial representation, touching the subject of slavery, where by the laws of said State, District, or Territory, their circulation was prohibited," Whittier challenged in "A Summons":

> Men of the North-land! where's the manly spirit
>   Of the true-hearted and the unshackled gone?
> Sons of the old freemen, do we but inherit
>   Their names alone?
>
> Is the old Pilgrim spirit quenched within us,
>   Stoops the strong manhood of our souls so low,
> That Mammon's lure or Party's wile can win us
>   To silence now?
>
> .   .   .   .
>
> Sons of the best of fathers! will ye falter
>   With all they left ye perilled and at stake?
> Ho! once again on Freedom's holy altar
>   The fire awake.
>
> Prayer-strengthened for the trial, come together,
>   Put on the harness for the moral fight,
> And, with the blessing of your Heavenly Father,
>   Maintain the right!

But Whittier did not only write, he also continued to work ardently in other ways. He was elected vice-president of the New England Abolition Society; he was a member of the board and later secretary of the Essex County Anti-

Slavery Society. In 1836 he was re-elected to the Massachusetts legislature, but was warned by his physician that
his health could not stand the strain of another term. When
Abijah Thayer, now an editor in Philadelphia, invited his
former protégé to join him there in a less partisan journalistic
venture, Whittier replied that he could not in conscience
even seem to desert the unpopular crusade in which he was
engaged, "especially as I have been somewhat active . . . and
as my *apparent* withdrawal from it might be construed very
unfavorably to the cause as well as to myself." He regarded
"the contest now going on as of vital interest to the welfare
of mankind, not in our country alone, but in all the world.
It is a struggle for the right of man everywhere."[13]

In the spring of 1836, Whittier sold the family homestead
at Haverhill and moved with his mother and sister to a
cottage across the road from the Quaker meetinghouse in
Amesbury. Beginning in May, he again assumed editorship
of the *Gazette*; but he was so forthright in editorial comment
that subscribers diminished and his resignation was required.
He continued active in politics and in antislavery activities,
which to him were the same. He continued also, and with
more than ordinary courage, to expose himself to the violence
of mobs which opposed reform and reformers. When the
Essex County Anti-Slavery Society met in July, 1837, at
Newburyport, the meeting was broken up by a gang of toughs,
beating tin pans, blowing raucously on horns, and throwing
the inevitable rotten eggs. Whittier admitted with wry humor
that he left the premises precipitously "at an undignified trot."

Soon he was called to larger participation. The spring of
1837 found him in New York as one of the corresponding
secretaries of the American Anti-Slavery Society. As such,
Whittier helped edit the *Emancipator* and the *Anti-Slavery
Record,* wrote personal appeals to public men, distributed
petitions to the Congress, opposed interstate slave trade and
the annexation of Texas, but wholeheartedly endorsed immediate emancipation in the District of Columbia. Though
much of the work could be done at his leisure at his quarters
across the river in Brooklyn, Whittier's health once more
defeated him; by the end of the summer of 1837 he had
retired to his New Hampshire home.

While Whittier worked in New York, a collection of his political poems was brought together in Boston by Isaac Knapp, publisher of the *Liberator,* and published as *Poems Written during the Progress of the Abolition Question in the United States, between the Years 1830 and 1838* (1837). The poet must have known of the project, but he seems to have had little to do with either the selection or the editing of the poems included in the volume. He apologized for it as "full of errors and ridiculously printed, merely for abolition purposes."[14] His estrangement from a wide or purely literary audience because of partisan activities was now clearly defined. "It is to be regretted," said Knapp in introduction to this volume, "as a loss to American literature, that one so highly gifted as a poet should devote so little time to poetic labors. . . . But," he continued, "he may derive satisfaction from the idea, that his labors for the honor of his nation, in a nobler sense, will ultimately give freedom and life to her literature—now withering beneath the soul-enslaving censorship of a public, who exact of an author that he shall not *unreservedly* name the very name of freedom."

Late in the fall of 1838 Whittier moved to Philadelphia to work on the editorial staff of the *National Inquirer,* an outspoken antislavery periodical to which he had long been a contributor. By March, 1839, the name of the paper was changed to the *Pennsylvania Freeman,* with Whittier in full editorial control. His complete energies were dedicated now to the task before him. Quietly, but with determination, he applied himself to another round of persuasive propaganda. Sometimes his judgment was wrong, and he listened too credulously to lurid recitals of evils perpetrated among the cotton fields south of the Mason-Dixon line. Early in 1838, for example, he had prepared a *Narrative of James Williams, an American Slave,* a hair-raising account of torture and cruelty which ran through six editions within eight months, and created such a storm of indignation in the South as a "foul fester of falsehood" that, some of its details being unsupported by corroborative testimony, it was withdrawn from publication.[15]

Whittier was not at his best, even in *Justice and Expediency,* in presenting an objective indictment. His mind slipped easily from the conceptual to the pictorial, from logical exposition to lurid detail. When, in an early editorial in the *Freeman*, he sought to explain "The True Character of Slavery" as a violation of the integrity of "the entire man," he was less successful than when he wrote of fetters clanking, whips lashing blood-stained backs, and dusky females forced to submit to horrid lusts of white masters. If he had not seen these things, he had read of them; his heart was stirred. That some slaveholders were or were said to be kindly men, was beside the point, a kind of "ecclesiastical hair-splitting," said Whittier: "the praying slaveholder does more to uphold the system than the swearing one" because he "gives it credit and countenance by his direct participation." And the clergyman who defended slavery was "the most dangerous enemy with which Christianity has to contend."[16]

Though familiar with all the arguments against slavery—that it was finally impractical and uneconomical, that it sapped the vitality of the white workingman, and that the slaver inevitably became himself enslaved—Whittier gave essential credence to one conviction: slavery was contrary to the will of God. Thus he reduced the problem to simplest, incontrovertible terms. It was neither law nor custom which empowered one man to enslave another: it was the voice of Satan which tempted man, just as it was satanic vice in him which allowed man to listen and be persuaded to consider "rational, immortal beings as articles of traffic, vendible commodities, merchantable property," and to tear "without scruple the infant from the mother, the wife from the husband, the parent from the child."[17]

As he wrote for the *Pennsylvania Freeman*, Whittier's appeal was frankly to the emotions; for people all over the United States must be stirred, as he had been, by the gothic horrors of clanking chains, foul imprisonments, and lacerations of soul and body. That he had known these things only by report and the extension of his sympathetic imagination did not seem important. What was important was that people everywhere should hear, as he had heard, of the soul-scarring effects of human slavery. The affective quality of such a poem as "The Farewell of a Virginia Slave Mother to her

Daughters Sold into Southern Bondage" was more important
than its excellence as verse:

> Gone, gone,—sold and gone,
> To the rice-swamp dank and lone
> Where the slave-whip ceaseless swings,
> Where the noisome insect stings,
> Where the fever demon strews
> Poison with the falling dews,
> Where the sickly sunbeams glare
> Through the hot and noisome air;
> Gone, gone,—sold and gone,
> To the rice-swamp dank and lone,
> From Virginia's hills and waters;
> Woe is me, my stolen daughters!

In addition to performing duties as editor, Whittier was
a staff officer working behind scenes who determined policy
and was often now in opposition to William Lloyd Garrison
who advocated meeting violence with violence by developing
the abolition forces into a combative, hard-hitting organiza-
tion which would refuse to turn the other cheek when mobs
rose against them. Sometimes it seemed to Whittier and his
friends that Garrison would even risk a war which would
divide the nation. In addition, Garrison was an all-outer who
thought that other reforms—temperance, the betterment of
prisons, even the rights of women—should be effected all at
once and by whatever means. To Whittier this aspiration
distracted energies from his own main objective; further-
more, he believed that his contemporaries, shown the truth,
would move in conscience toward abolition.

During his residence in Philadelphia, Whittier moved
quietly among Quaker circles, making new friends, perhaps
even falling in love. Through all his life he was attractive to
women, and he enjoyed their company as much as they
enjoyed his. He must have seemed to them what can be called
a safe man, dignified, thoughtful, sensitive, and not particularly strong, except in spirit. Some probably did think of
marrying him, and there is evidence that he more than once

thought of marrying one of them. The precariousness of his health, his poverty, and his responsibility for the support of his mother and sister have been set forth as reasons for his lifelong bachelorhood. Most people are willing to let the matter rest there, respecting Whittier's modest reticence in talking about this kind of personal attachment.[18] He was, almost above everything else, a gentle man.

III *Passive Resistance*

In May, 1838, he offered a resolution to the meeting in New York of the American Anti-Slavery Society that physical force should never be used by members of that group, whatever the violence of their enemies against them. Before Thoreau and before Gandhi, he pleaded the Quaker conviction that effective, passive resistance to oppressive measures needed only a determined will and the assurance that the cause was just; without violence, right inevitably would prevail. Whittier's resolution did not carry, but it effectively set him apart from the firebrands of his party.

Violence soon surrounded him. Whittier returned to Philadelphia for the ceremonious opening on May 15 of Pennsylvania Hall, which had been erected by public subscription to provide a center where "principles of Liberty, and Equality of Civil Rights, could be freely discussed, and the evils of slavery fearlessly portrayed." The editorial offices of the *Pennsylvania Freeman* had been moved into the new building, and Whittier had prepared a dedicatory poem to the new "resting-place for hunted Liberty," where men might speak "unshackled and unawed." Two days later a mob set fire to the building, destroying the office of the *Pennsylvania Freeman* "and with it," said Whittier, "all my books and papers." He continued publication from makeshift quarters, and he asserted in an editorial the next day: "The beautiful temple consecrated to Liberty has been offered a smoking sacrifice to the Demon of Slavery. In the heart of the city a flame has gone up to Heaven. It will be seen from Maine to Georgia. In its red and lurid light, men will see more clearly than ever the black abominations of the fiend at whose instigation it was kindled."

It is sometimes difficult to remember what bravely dedicated men these early abolitionists were and that Whittier
was among them. Mobs pursued them through the streets, and
they often had to travel disguised at night from one village to
another. On the evening when Pennsylvania Hall was burned
and his office with it, Whittier, disguising himself by putting
on the long white coat of a compositor in the printing shop,
joined the crowd clamoring about the building and daring the
editor to come forth; and he even joined in their cries of
"Hang him! Hang him!" Thus, testified one of his associates,
Whittier was capable of "guilefully deceiving his foes and
saving his life." Scorned by men considered the best in the
community and threatened by mobs made up of the worst,
struggling toward truth through dark storms of human hatred,
Whittier asked prayerfully in verses "To the Memory of
Thomas Shipley," a fellow abolitionist, martyred to the cause,

> for that hidden strength which can
> Nerve unto death the inner man.

He asked for gentleness and understanding and

> for that spirit, meek and mild,
>   Derided, spurned, yet uncomplaining;
> By man deserted and reviled,
>   Yet faithful to its trust remaining.
> Still prompt and resolute to save
> From scourge and chain the hunted slave;
> Unwavering in the Truth's defence,
>   Even where the fires of Hate are burning,
> The unquailing eye of innocence
>   Alone upon oppression turning!

At a time like this, when Freedom—Whittier invariably
capitalized words like Freedom, Truth, Love, and Hate—was
beset on all sides by men who would stain her spotless garments, other men must marshall themselves around her as
guardians of her honor. He spoke of "Moral Warfare," and
he used martial, quite un-Quakerish terms:

> In God's own might
> We gird us for the coming fight,

> And, strong in him, whose cause is ours
> In conflict with unholy powers,
> We grasp the weapons He has given,—
> The Light, the Truth, and Love of Heaven.

God's word—truth, sharpened by love—was weapon enough, capable of putting all evil to rout. Whittier did not lift his own arm in anger, nor did he suggest that anyone actually do battle, even against satanic slaveholders in the South

> Where the cant of Democracy dwells on the lips
> Of the forgers of fetters, and wielders of whips!
> Where "chivalric" honor means really no more
> Than scourging of women, and robbing the poor.

Words like these from "Ritner," verses written in praise of Pennsylvania's liberal governor, brought retaliatory words from proslavery quarters, words as bitterly recriminatory as those Whittier hurled against them.

The vehemence of attacks against him seemed proof to Whittier not only that the cause was just but that it was gaining ground. "The politicians," he wrote, "are abusing us in their filthy papers; and dirty penny-sheets, with most outrageous caricatures . . . are hawked daily about the streets." His own newspaper, he confided to his sister, was "beginning to attract attention, and I should not think it strange if it got pretty essentially mobbed before the summer is out." But the strain of work and worry became increasingly great on him. "I wish," he wrote in August, "I could escape the duties of an editor for a month or so. My health needs it."[19] In October, when he did retire for recuperation at his cottage at Amesbury, he sent contributions to the *Freeman* by mail until April, 1839, when he returned once more to Philadelphia.

During his absence the first collected volume of his poems over which Whittier exercised editorial control was issued by Joseph Healy, the financial agent of the Anti-Slavery Society of Pennsylvania. Called simply *Poems by John G. Whittier,* its contents were mainly, though not entirely, made up of verses which called for an emotional response to the failure of freedom to spread its benison to all men. What has been called the keynote of Whittier's career as a reformer was struck as he quoted on the title page Coleridge's brave affirmation of his responsibilities as a man of letters to truth:

"There is a time to keep silence," said Solomon. But when I proceeded to the fourth chapter of Ecclesiastes, "and considered all the oppressions that are done under the sun, and beheld the tears of such as are oppressed, and they had no comforter; and on the side of the oppressors there was power," I concluded that this was *not* the time to keep silence; for Truth should be spoke at all times, but more especially at those times when to speak the Truth is dangerous.

Whittier's active participation in antislavery activities, however, was almost over. In July, 1839, he surrendered the drudgery of editorial work for a few weeks of strenuous holiday—a recruiting tour through western Pennsylvania. Later in that month he attended a national antislavery convention in Albany, where he met with reformers who, like himself, disapproved of the violent measures advocated by Garrison and his followers. Then he retired, ill and discouraged, to Amesbury, where he remained with his mother and sister until early fall. Returning once more to Philadelphia, he resumed active editorial responsibilities, but the pressure of work was finally too much for him. On February 20, 1840, he published a farewell editorial in the *Pennsylvania Freeman*. He planned to attend a world-wide antislavery convention to be held a few months later in London, but his doctors forbade it.

Instead he lived quietly at the cottage in Amesbury, and he left the calm and the ministrations of home only to attend the annual summer meeting of the Friends at Newport. People began to whisper that he had left Philadelphia and the abolition movement because of differences of opinion with others among its leaders. But Whittier denied this with quiet insistence, affirming his confidence "in the justice of the cause, in the beauty and excellence of its principles, and in the wisdom and expediency of its prominent measures." "I am still," he said, "as far as my failing health admits of, ready to do and suffer, if need be, for abolitionism."[20]

CHAPTER 3

The Voice of New England, 1840-1865

A *silent, shy, peace-loving man,*
He seemed no fiery partisan
To hold his way against the public frown,
The ban of Church and State, the fierce mob's
                                        hounding down.

For while he wrought with strenuous will
    The work his hands had found to do,
He heard the fitful music still
    Of winds that out of dream-land blew.
                        —"The Tent on the Beach"

HOWEVER IMPRUDENT may be the attempt to explain any man's motives, particularly when time and a confusion of testimony intervenes, it does seem probable that, whether he recognized it or not, an important reason for Whittier's retirement from active antislavery work in 1840 may have been difference in opinion with some of its other leaders. For one thing, Whittier had wished that Garrison and his good-hearted associates would concentrate upon abolition and not dissipate their fire by directing it at the same time toward other matters of reform. For another, he wanted them to take more direct political action; not holding themselves aloof from party, they were to work directly on the power of votes, peacefully cast, to effect correction. Ballots, not bullets—he wished some of his associates were less bellicose. If violence were to be met with violence— Satan's work, Whittier said, with Satan's work—his Quaker conscience could permit him no part in the enterprise. Argument was one thing, but fists or clubs or firearms were quite another. One did not do battle in a literal sense for opinions; one stated them cogently and with all the emotional force he could provide, relying on the convincing power of truth.

Whittier's attitude was little changed, therefore, from what it had been six years before: slavery must go, but without the use of force. "For the principle and practice of slavery," he had said, "I entertain no other feelings than those of disgust and abhorrence. A free citizen of that state which rocked of old the cradle of American liberty, I have a right to express those feelings. For the two millions of my enslaved and outraged fellow beings, I feel sympathy which I shall not seek to disguise—a sympathy which should belong to every lover of freedom—every friend of suffering humanity, and for their relief I am ready to join in any measure *political* or otherwise, which is sanctioned by Religion and Humanity, and which involves no violation of the American Constitution, or the laws of my own State. . . . But deeply as I detest the system of slavery, my political principles forbid me to seek its overthrow by advocating an unconstitutional intervention with the Slave-holding States."[1]

Perhaps there are other and simpler reasons for Whittier's withdrawal at thirty-three from active but poorly paying participation in reform. "My relish for poetry," he wrote, "is as strong as ever—but the pleasure of composition has in a great degree ceased. It has all become task work." During the past eight years he had given himself completely to the cause of abolition; he had written from the heart with little concern for his pocketbook or even for the damage which his partisan rhymes did to his literary reputation. "Now, if my health holds, I must do something for myself, and labor with head, or hands if necessary, for the maintenance of that pecuniary independence, which every honorable mind must seek for."[2]

He was tired, he was discouraged, and he needed money— these facts are plain. The migraine headaches, the nervous collapse, the palpitations of the heart which accompanied each retreat to Whittier's Essex County home, whatever their physical base, seem almost certainly to have been symptoms also of a mind not at peace with itself. Some have wondered whether Whittier's chaste bachelor existence, his devotion to his mother and sister, and his lifelong series of platonic friendships with other admiring ladies may not in some Freudian sense provide clues to his disorders and his retreats. Others have underscored the conflict between his Quaker quietness and his aggressive campaigning for reform. Still others suggest an artist's conscience disturbed because he put his talents out for hire.[3] Speculations such as these are possibly as impolite as they are unimportant. Perhaps, like Thoreau only a little later, he was a village boy, unhappy away from home.

Return to Amesbury did not mean complete retirement. For the next quarter-century—or even longer—Whittier continued quietly active in politics and reform. When both Whigs and Democrats in his congressional district nominated men for the House of Representatives from whom he could not obtain pledges in behalf of emancipation, he prevented the election of either by allowing himself to be presented in several successive contests, and he attracted enough votes so that neither candidate of the major parties could acquire the majority which was then required. At each trial, votes for Whittier increased, until in December, 1843, seeing himself in danger of winning, he threw his influence behind the Whig candidate when he had obtained from that gentleman certain promises of support for antislavery measures. He corresponded with John Quincy Adams, who spoke as forthrightly in Congress for reform as Whittier thought all men should. He struck up a friendship with Charles Sumner whose political career he watched with increasing admiration. He continued in correspondence with antislavery leaders, and he participated faithfully in sober deliberations at Quaker meetings.

Men of persuasive power like Henry Wadsworth Longfellow, whose *Poems of Slavery* appeared in 1842, and of reputation like Ralph Waldo Emerson were now beginning to speak out; and Whittier wished they had spoken earlier. After Emerson had made a forthright plea for emancipation in Concord in 1844, the Quaker quietly remarked that it had not seemed right that "while we were struggling against the popular current, mobbed, hounded, denounced from the legislative forum, cursed from the pulpit, sneered at by wealth and aristocracy, such a man as Ralph Waldo Emerson should be brooding over his pleasant philosophies, writing his quaint and beautiful essays, in his retirement on the banks of the Concord." But Whittier welcomed him "into our dusty and toil-worn ranks, where every man does battle with whatsoever weapon his hands find."[4]

I *Mending a Reputation*

His own pen continued to scratch out songs of freedom, but Whittier wrote now as often of the familiar hills and fields and streams of his native county, of the Merrimack River which flowed past Amesbury to the sea, and of the memories and legends of which these scenes reminded him. During these quiet years, he turned to old themes, telling something of the legend of Acadia in "St. John," of the founding of Nantucket in a ballad called "The Exiles," of old-time Quaker persecution at Salem in "Cassandra Southwick," and of Indian legend in "The Bridal of Pennacock."

Verses done in this manner were brought together in a volume called *Lays of My Home* and published by William D. Ticknor of Boston in June, 1843—the first of Whittier's books to be issued by the distinguished firm that, under successive names, was to bring out each of the authorized editions of his writings. Whittier chose the poems for this volume with care; discarding the ephemeral and the patently imitative, he selected those of which he approved and continued to approve as he supervised later editions of his verse. "I suppose," he had written to James T. Fields, who was associated with Ticknor, "there is already an abundance of poetry in the market, but a wish to preserve a few floating pieces of mine, and to favor some personal friends induces me to think of publishing a small collection. . . . I want it printed in first rate style or not at all."[5] Removed from partisan journalism, he was eager to mend his poetical reputation by separating chaff from wheat. He must have derived satisfaction when hardly a year later a collection of his *Ballads and Other Poems* was published in London in a series which had included volumes by Bryant, Emerson, and Longfellow.

Whittier realized the difference between his poems of place, legend, and sentiment and those of persuasion which were printed and reprinted in antislavery journals; and he was eager to have the distinction between them recognized by his readers. As long, however, as freedom was challenged, he would continue to write such poems as he wrote now of "The Christian Slave":

> Hoarse, horrible, and strong,
> Rises to Heaven that agonizing cry,
> Filling the arches of the hollow sky,
> How long, O God, how long.

He would also persist in expressing his Quaker disdain for the saber-rattling South in poems like "Massachusetts to Virginia":

> We hear thy threats, Virginia! thy stormy words
> and high
> Swell harshly on the Southern winds which melt
> along our sky;
> Yet, not one brown hard hand forgoes its honest
> labor here,
> No hewer of our mountain oaks suspends his
> axe in fear.

Because Virginia scoffs at freedom, he said, must Massachusetts then turn from her concern with freedom and truth, or her assurance that they would prevail?

> We wage no war, we lift no arm, we fling no
> torch within
> The fire-damps of quaking mine beneath your
> soul of sin;
> We leave ye with your bondmen, to wrestle
> while ye can,
> With the strong upward tendencies and godlike
> soul of man.

In "The Song of the Vermonters" written perhaps ten years before in memory of brave resistance during the American

Revolution, but apparently now first printed, he seemingly struck a more martial note:

> Hail—all to the borders! Vermonters come down,
> With your breeches of deer-skin, and jackets
>   of brown;
> With your red woolen caps, and your moccasins,
>   come
> To the gathering summons of trumpet and gun.

For two months in the fall of 1841 Whittier served as corresponding editor of the *American and Foreign Anti-Slavery Reporter*; and, toward the end of that year, he was temporary editor of the *Emancipator and Free American*, published in Boston. His health allowed no permanent editorial commitment; but, since his pocketbook was lean, he wrote unashamedly for what money he could get from such popular magazines as the literary *Democratic Review*, the *Knickerbocker Magazine*, and James Russell Lowell's *Pioneer*. His voice even now was beginning to be accepted as part of the increasingly familiar New England choir which included Longfellow, Holmes, Lowell and Emerson—but Whittier was never to be completely of their group.

He not only welcomed Longfellow's tentative commitment to abolition but tried without success to tempt the Cambridge poet to more active participation. Whimsical Dr. Holmes was too mild: he admitted slavery "a dreadful business," but he was scornful of vituperative abolition eloquence and quite frankly said that he found "nothing so flat and unprofitable as weakly flavored" abolition verse. Only Lowell, who was more receptive to encouragement, did lend his facile talent briefly to the cause. More than any of these literary contemporaries, Whittier was a profoundly sincere, dedicated man. Whatever its quality, his verse reached more readers than that of any of the others. And by the 1840's critics who had objected to his unashamed use of words as weapons were beginning to recognize him as a poet who, when he would, wrote as pleasantly well as any of his native contemporaries.

II *Wizardry of Mechanism—and Humanity*

In the summer of 1844 Whittier moved to the busy manu-
facturing town of Lowell, where he remained for almost eight
months as editor of the *Middlesex Standard*. One result of
this sojourn was a volume of eighteen prose essays—most
of which had appeared in his newspaper—which was published in July, 1845, as *The Stranger in Lowell*. The new
industrialism which altered the familiar rustic face of New
England both charmed and appalled him. Even the rivers
were "tamed and subdued to the purposes of man, chained
to slavish subjection to the wizard of mechanism" in this
"millennium of steam-engines and cotton-mills." In the fac-
tories women worked side by side with men—a good thing,
Whittier thought. But since their average work day extended through twelve and a half hours, their health and
family life both suffered. Whittier thought that ten hours of
work a day would be greatly preferable, even if wages had
to be lowered to make this possible. It satisfied his democratic
notions that in this new world of machines there was not
room for the idle, aristocratic gentlemen; nor was there room
for any man who was a loafer: "Work here is the patron
saint" and "gain is the great, all absorbing object."[6]

Like Thoreau, who just now was beginning his experiment
in economy beside Walden Pond, Whittier argued that labor,
"graduated to man's simple wants, necessities, and unper-
verted tastes, is doubtless well; but all beyond this is weariness to flesh and spirit." He wondered if the machine,
"grinding on, each in its iron harness," was *really* "raising
us, by wheel and pulley, steam and waterpower, slowly up
that inclined plane from whose top stretches the broad table-
land of promise." As long as the "compatibility of mental cul-
tivation with bodily labor and the brotherhood and equality
of all the human family"[7] remained open questions, so long
would the ideal of democracy remain unrealized. Certainly
Whittier must have been reflecting the influence of Emerson's
Essays, the Second Series of which appeared while he was
in Lowell, when he wrote:

The truth is, our democracy lacks calmness and solidity, the repose and self-reliance which come of long habitude and settled convictions. We have not yet learned to wear its simple truths with the graceful ease and quiet air of un-solicitous assurance which the titled European does his social frictions. As a people, we do not feel and live out our great Declaration. We lack faith in man,—confidence in simple humanity, apart from its environments.

If Whittier did not write about these American character-istics in prose so well as Emerson or Thoreau did, he felt no less deeply than they—and with a compassionate humility which glows warmly beside their more austere precision. "I confess," he said, "a special dislike of disfigured faces, osten-tatious displays of piety, pride aping humility." He could not find it in his heart to condemn even workingmen Sabbath-breakers "for seeking on this their sole day of leisure the needful influences of social enjoyment, unrestrained exercise, and fresh air." Asceticism, moroseness, self-torture, or ingrati-tude for the blessings showered in abundance on men—these, he thought, look "sadly out of place in a believer of the glad evangel of the New Testament."

For it was in the life and teachings of Jesus that Whittier found solace, inspiration, and example for a breadth of human kindness which could not be found in the words or attitudes of even the best of his contemporaries: Garrison's anger blurred the sureness of his vision; Thoreau's *Walden*, Whittier thought, was "capital reading, but very wicked and heathenish"; and Emerson seemed satisfied to speak only of "the mystery of the glory around us" better than any other. Whittier preferred the simpler humanity of the man from Nazareth, who "broke bread with the poor despised publican," who "spoke compassionate words to the sin-sick Magdalene," who had regard "even to the merely animal wants of the multitude in the wilderness," who "frowned upon none of life's simple and natural pleasures":

The burden of His gospel was love; and in life and word
He taught evermore the divided and scattered children of
one great family that only as they drew near each other

could they approach Him who was their common centre; and that while no ostentation of prayers nor rigid observance of ceremonies could elevate man to heaven, the simple exercise of love, in thought and action, could bring heaven down to man. To weary and restless spirits He brought the great truth, that happiness consists in making others happy.[9]

III Growing Popularity and Innovations

This faith, so simply compelling, runs in refrain through everything which Whittier wrote; and it was embellished by his love of the wild beauty and quiet harmonies of his New England landscape—the "grand and glorious forest, broken by lakes and crossed by great rivers, intersected by a thousand streams more beautiful than those which the Old World has given to song and romance."[10] As Whittier's name became better known—not only as a partisan poet, but as a sympathetic celebrator of native history in verse and prose—a growing demand for his writings resulted during the next five years in a variety of volumes which set forth the increasing diversity of his interests. In 1846 *Voices of Freedom*, another book of antislavery poems and one virtually identical with the *Poems* of 1838, was published in Philadelphia, apparently again without Whittier's supervision. Essays on the folk background of his native countryside, which he had contributed to the *United States Magazine and Democratic Review*, were collected in January, 1847, as *The Supernaturalism of New England*.

A handsome new edition of the *Poems*, which brought together what Whittier considered the better work in his previous volumes, plus thirty-five poems "now first collected," was issued in Boston in 1848. More substantial than any which had preceded it—one hundred and six poems in 384 pages—and handsomely illustrated by Hammatt Billings, designer of the Pilgrim Monument at Plymouth, this was certainly a book fit to set beside the illustrated editions of Longfellow and Bryant which had been recently appearing. Perhaps more important, for what seems to have been the first time in his career, Whittier made money on a volume of verse—five hundred dollars for the copyright and a royalty of two and a half per cent. Again he apologized in words

drawn from Coleridge for his deviation from the strict poetic
way:

> "Was it right,
> "While my unnumbered brethren toiled and bled,
> "That I should dream away th' intrusted hours
> "On rose leaf beds, pampering the coward heart
> "With feelings all too delicate for use?"

Not only duty but a sense of new areas for poetry which
the New World and its democratic ways offered now enticed
Whittier away from conventional verse subjects. In the summer of 1850 he presented his *Songs of Labor,* which antici-
pate but stand shoddily beside Walt Whitman's celebration
of the dignity and worth of physical toil and of working men.
These poems, on "The Ship Builders," "The Shoemakers,"
"The Drovers," "The Fishermen," "The Huskers," and "The
Lumbermen"—all good New England vocations—were written,
said Whittier, for "working, *acting,* rather than *thinking*
people. I wish to invest labor with some degree of beauty."

When in January, 1847, the National and Foreign Anti-
Slavery Society established in Washington a weekly paper
named the *National Era,* Whittier was invited to become a
corresponding editor; he could remain in Amesbury and send
what contributions he would by mail. For the next ten years—
until the first issue of the *Atlantic Monthly* appeared late in
1857—virtually his entire literary output was devoted to that
paper. Sometimes as many as five or six contributions appeared in a single issue—and, in all, more than a hundred
original poems and almost three hundred prose pieces which
included editorials, literary essays, sketches, and reports.
Some of his best remembered verse appeared there: the
dramatic narrative of "Maud Muller"; the fine descriptive
poem, "The Hill Top"; and his terrible denunciation of Daniel
Webster's apparent defection from the cause of justice,
"Ichabod." Nothing that Whittier wrote stirred readers so
effectively as Harriet Beecher's Stowe's *Uncle Tom's Cabin*
which appeared as a serial in the *National Era* in 1851 and
1852, and nothing of his reached the polished excellence of
Nathaniel Hawthorne's "The Great Stone Face" which ap-

peared early in 1850; but the cumulative impression of Whittier's work was greater perhaps than that of any other.

Again, he did too much; he wrote too fast; and his health and his spirits gave way. When he had contributed to the *National Era* hardly more than two years, he confessed to a friend: "I feel a growing disinclination to pen and ink. Over-worked and tired by long weary years of the anti-slavery struggle, I want mental rest. I have already lived a long life, if thought and action constitute it. I have crowded into a few years what should have been given to many."[11]

But he kept doggedly at the task to which, he thought, duty called him. Collections of his writings continued to be called for: *The Chapel of the Hermits and Other Poems*, composed principally of his contributions in verse to the *National Era*, appeared in 1853; *Literary Recreations and Miscellanies*, a collection of prose reprinted mostly from *The Stranger in Lowell* and the columns of the *Era*, in 1854; and *The Panorama and Other Poems*, in which "Maud Muller" and "The Barefoot Boy" first appeared within the covers of a book, in 1856. A year later, Ticknor and Fields in Boston issued *The Poetical Works of John Greenleaf Whittier* in two volumes in their "Blue and Gold" series which also included similar editions of the poems of Longfellow and Tennyson. Previous to this edition, Whittier's verse had been scattered through several small volumes; "and you have not," wrote James T. Fields, "had a fair chance at the poetic market. Now we hope you will have a wider hearing."[12]

Opportunity for wider hearing came most surely with the establishment in 1857 of the *Atlantic Monthly* by Fields, Lowell, Oliver Wendell Holmes, and others of the literary group which centered in Boston. Whittier joined them, along with Emerson, Motley, Longfellow, and several more, at a dinner meeting during the summer at which plans for the new periodical were discussed. Lowell was appointed its editor, and Holmes gave the new periodical a name. When the splendid first issue appeared in November, literature in the United States entered a new era of continuing excellence; and a new era began for Whittier also. Though he continued through 1859 as contributing editor of the *National Era*, he contributed less to it and increasingly more to the *Atlantic Monthly*—six poems, for example, appeared in the *Era* in 1858, and six in the *Atlantic*: in 1859, three in the *Era* and six in the *Atlantic*. Because it was liberal and yet devotedly literary, and also perhaps because it paid higher fees, the new magazine offered him more freedom, better and more dignified company among its contributors, and an infinitely larger discriminating audience. During the next few years some of Whittier's best remembered verse appeared in its pages, side by side with that of Emerson, Longfellow, Lowell, and Holmes—things like "Skipper Ireson's Ride," "Telling the Bees," and "Barbara Frietchie." Measured by quality, the collection of thirty-six poems in *Home Ballads and Other Poems*, which Ticknor and Fields published in the summer of 1860, was the best which Whittier had yet offered.

IV *War and the Quaker*

As war between the North and the South appeared inevitable, Whittier drew more quietly into himself. His mother had died in 1857, and his sister Elizabeth had become a semi-invalid. He was not well—reading or writing for more than a brief period brought on the blinding misery of migraine. His usefulness as an editor of the *National Era* seemed at an end; for the cause seemed surely won, though not as he would have it won. "I have never," he said, "written a poem in praise or favor of war." It saddened and distressed him: "Only think of it," he wrote in dismay to a friend, "Democracy divided against itself." He would preserve the Union, but only if "it could be *the* Union of our fathers," not compromised by concessions to evil. He shuddered still at thought of violence—"as friends of peace as well as Freedom, as believers in the Sermon on the Mount, we dare not lend *any* countenance to such attempts as those at Harpers Ferry." What a sad tragedy these events seemed. "I feel a deep sympathy for John Brown," said Whittier, "but deplore from my heart his rash and insane attempt. It injures the cause he sought to serve."[13]

But Whittier bowed to the inevitability of war: "We prayed and hoped; but still with awe, The coming of the sword we saw." He convinced himself that the reckless unconcern for human rights of slaveholding states made necessary "whatever painful duty may be imposed upon the government." It may be the will of God, said Whittier, as if with a sigh of righteous resignation, that slavery shall perish through the folly and crime of the South. But, he wrote, "I have never been an enemy of the South," only of slavery.[14] When action began on the battlefields, he watched not only in anguish but with continuing strong faith that what his northern countrymen fought for was just, and that God's will would bring them through suffering to victory.

His Quaker convictions denied him any part in the conflict; but he asserted in a circular printed at Amesbury in June, 1861, entitled *To Members of the Society of Friends*: "We have no right to ask or expect an exemption from the chastisement which Divine Providence is inflicting upon the nation. Steadily and faithfully maintaining our testimony against war, we owe it to the cause of truth, to show that exalted heroism and generous self-sacrifice are not incompatible with our pacific principles."[15] Quakers might, as Walt Whitman did, visit the sick and the wounded; and they could also tighten their belts to greater economies so that extra funds could be available to help relieve the miseries of orphans and widows and people displaced by war from their homes. Whittier's writings against slavery had driven the peace which he sought from the land. Such a result, he said in "Astrea at the Capitol," was

> Not as we hoped; but what are we?
>   Above our broken dreams and plans
>   God lays, with wiser hand than man's,
> The corner-stones of liberty.
>
> I cavil not with Him: the voice
>   That freedom's blessed gospel tells
>   Is sweet to me as silver bells,
> Rejoicing!—yea, I will rejoice.

No battle songs came from Whittier's pen, only words of encouragement, as he waited, he said "beneath the furnace blast" for the inevitable triumph of right which would "mould anew the nation." He wrote prayerfully for "grace to keep our faith and patience":

> safe on freedom's vantage-ground
> Our feet are planted: Let us there remain
> In unrevengeful calm, no means untried
> Which truth can sanction.

As he and his fellows watched the fratricidal fight, "sad spectators," said Whittier, "of a suicide," he asked in an adaptation of "Luther's Hymn" (*"Ein feste Burg ist unser Gott"*) that

> God give us grace
> Each in his place
> To bear his lot
> And, murmuring not,
> Endure and want and labor!

Only occasionally, as when he heard the church bells of Amesbury ring to greet passage of the constitutional amendment abolishing slavery, did his voice rise as in "Laus Deo" above prayerful resignation. "Praise God," he said now in exultation, "It is done!"

> Ring, O bells!
> Every stroke exulting tells
> Of the burial hour of crime.
> Loud and long, that all may hear,
> Ring for every listening ear
> Of Eternity and Time!
>
> . . . .
>
> Send the song of praise abroad!
> With the sound of broken chains
> Tell the nation that He reigns,
> Who alone is Lord and God!

Late in 1863 Whittier collected many of these poems written in heartache amid the conflict in a volume called *In War Time,* which compares poorly with Herman Melville's collection of war poems in *Battle Pieces* or with Walt Whitman's in *Drum Taps*. Whittier's were journeyman's verses, tired and discouraged as he was as he looked in "agony of prayer" through "a clouded sky" over a "land red with judgments" but was upheld by his faith that "the war-field's crimson stain" might symbolize "the blood-red dawn of Freedom's day." But as he saw also what happened to people around him—"the rapacity of contractors and office-holders, and the brutal ferocious prejudice against the poor blacks"—he wondered "whether we really deserve success in this terrible war." Sometimes, as when Abraham Lincoln stood staunchly against all opposition in support of the Emancipation Proclamation, Whittier's spirits rose. "We are living," he thought then, "in a grand time; one year now is worth a dozen of the years of our ancestors."[16]

Even among the strains and anxieties of war, he mused often in milder keys, with songs of nature's beauty and the retelling of old legends in verse to "relieve the storm-stunned ear" of his countrymen. When in 1861 he submitted an old New England tale of faithful love called "Amy Wentworth" to the *Atlantic Monthly*, he explained that he had not touched the story

<blockquote>
with warmer tints in vain,
If, in this dark, sad year, it steals one thought from pain.
</blockquote>

In dedicating "The Countess," a simple ballad of lovers' true devotion, to his Quaker friend Elias Weld, Whittier admitted sadly that

<blockquote>
Today when truth and falsehood speak their words
Through hot-lipped cannon and the teeth of swords,
Listening with quickened heart and ear intent
To each sharp clause of that stern argument,
I still can hear at times a softer note
Of the old pastoral music round me float,
While through the hot gleam of our civil strife
Looms the green mirage of a simpler life.
</blockquote>

CHAPTER 4

At Sundown, 1865-1892

No time is this for hands long overworn
To task their strength; and (unto Him be praise
Who giveth quietness!) the stress and strain
Of years that did the work of centuries
Have ceased, and we can draw our breath once more
Freely and full. So, as yon harvesters
Make glad their nooning underneath the elms
With tale and riddle and old snatch of song,
I lay aside grave themes, and idly turn
The leaves of Memory's sketch-book, dreaming o'er
Old summer pictures of the quiet hills
And human life, as quiet, at their feet.

—"Among the Hills"

WHEN ELIZABETH WHITTIER died after months of painful illness in September, 1864, her brother's thoughts turned again to older, better times of quiet comfort on the homestead farm. A few weeks after her death, he wrote to a friend: "The woods I find still have power to charm and soothe me. My health is better, but I cannot write. I busy myself with my garden."[1] His name—along with those of Emerson, Bryant, Longfellow, Lowell, Holmes, and others—was included in the summer of 1864 in a bill which Charles Sumner introduced to the Senate for the formation of a National Academy of Literature and Art. His Amesbury cottage swarmed with visitors who came to offer condolences or to do homage to the laureate of what seemed now a righteous and victorious cause. Whittier responded with quiet graciousness, but he was tired and increasingly reminiscent. When the war ended, he breathed prayerfully in "The Peace Autumn":

> Thank God for rest, where none molest,
>   And none can make afraid;
> For Peace that sits as Plenty's guest
>   Beneath the homestead shade!

I *The Changing Image*

Eight years before, James Russell Lowell, as editor of the *Atlantic Monthly*, had written Whittier: "I shall not let you rest till I have got a New England pastoral out of you." During the summer of 1865, Whittier wrote to Lowell's successor, James T. Fields: "I am writing a poem, 'Snow-Bound, a Winter Idyll,' a homely picture of old New England homes. If I ever finish it, I hope and trust it will be good." By October it was finished and in February, 1866, it was published. No poem since Longfellow's *Hiawatha* eleven years before did so well. Two months later, Fields wrote: "We can't keep the plaguey thing quiet. It goes and goes, and now, today, we are bankrupt again, not one being in the crib. I fear it will be impossible to get along without printing another batch."[2]

Another batch was printed, and still another, until *Snow-Bound* became a familiar household commodity and Whittier's passport to fame. The ten thousand dollars he received for it was the first considerable money which had come to him. It is a poem, as is *Hiawatha*, which today is better known and more often talked about than read; but during Whittier's lifetime and in the years immediately after, it ran through numerous editions. Its account of snug, family fireside contentment during winter days and evenings while snow and wind beat ineffectually against window pane and siding reminded countless readers of rural days which they had known but which, like the whaling adventures of which Melville wrote, were gone—and colored by memory to soft nostalgic recollection.

The public image of Whittier was now changing. "For twenty years I was shut out from the favor of booksellers and magazine editors," he explained. Now, approaching sixty, he was sure that "if my health allowed me to write, I could make money easily." He regretted nothing, however: "God has been good to me. I sometimes think I am about the richest man in the world . . . in loves and friendships, and the dear sense of kind remembrance and wishes flowing in upon me, peopling loneliness with forms of beauty, and displacing silence with sweet sounds." He had, as he wrote E. L. Godkin, editor of the *Nation*, no thirst for fame, no "poor ambitions and miserable jealousies" in pursuit of a literary reputation: "Up to a comparatively recent period my writings have been simply episodical, something apart from the real aim and object of my life; and whatever favor they have found with the public has come to me as a grateful surprise rather than as an expected reward. As I have never staked all on the chances of authorship, I have been spared the pain of disappointment and the temptation to envy those who, as men of letters, occupy a higher place than I have ever aspired to."[3]

Yet from this time until his death almost thirty years later, Whittier was increasingly a popular poet; he shared with Longfellow, Holmes, and Emerson a place in the familiar chorus of benign voices which cheered countrymen even beyond the limits of their native New England. Every volume which Whittier published—and they came in quick succession now—did satisfyingly well. He sat occasionally with his literary friends at the Saturday Club in Boston, but not so often as they wished; for he continued to enjoy, as Emerson is said to have once remarked to him, the simpler pleasures of poor health.

New England winters were particularly hard on him: "a wind of despair blows out of the bitter east." He worried about his illnesses and the lassitude they brought. "I have read and done nothing for a long time," he wrote in the early spring of 1867. "It seems a poor life of idleness, but I do not see how I can help it. I have had a great many strangers coming to look at me, and make speeches to me. It's a sort of thing to make one feel sadly mean and ridiculous. I envy the stout, steel-muscled farmers. I would rather chop wood than talk poetry with strangers. And indeed I think the life of a hard-working farmer or mechanic altogether more enviable than that of a writer or politician. Not but that poetry has been a great solace and refreshing, at times, to me; and I am grateful for the gift of verse that has been vouchsafed to me. But Plato and old Mr. Weller, I fear, are right in their discouragement of poets."[4]

The success of *Snow-Bound* was followed a year later by *The Tent on the Beach,* which Whittier thought was a better book; but few have agreed with him. Imagining that he and Fields and Bayard Taylor were camping on sand dunes by the Atlantic, he filled the volume with rhymed tales of older times, tales which were supposed to have been told as the three friends sat about their evening lamp. The interludes which join the poems are mildly discursive, sometimes auto-biographical, often almost apologetic; but, as Whittier explains his former excursions into propaganda and his notions of art as expressing something beyond "beauty for its own sake," these digressions are more interesting than the poems between which they appear. None of the small, moralistic narratives in the volume are remembered among Whittier's best, except perhaps the account in irregular blank verse of "Abraham Davenport," who in Puritan times stood erect, self-possessed, with rugged face, as witness that "simple duty hath no place for fear." But the volume sold amazingly well. Only a few weeks after it appeared, Whittier wrote to Fields: "Think of bagging this 'tent' of ours on an unsuspecting public at the rate of a thousand a day! This will never do. The swindle is awful. Barnum is a saint to us. I am bowed with a sense of guilt, ashamed to look an honest man in the face."[5]

During that winter Whittier was again seriously ill, as a slow, persistent fever burned all energy and appetite from him. "It will be a good while," he said early in 1868, "before I shall get up to even my usual very moderate degree of health and strength. It is a marvel to me that I am as well as I am."[6] Troubled by heart pains and insomnia, he lived quietly, receiving visitors, writing as he could. He was pleased to hear from Bayard Taylor, now in Europe, that Tennyson thought highly of his poems, and pleased also to learn that a Quaker college in Iowa had been named for him. But life

moved slowly for him now; more than half an hour's con-
tinuous work at his desk brought headaches again. It was
impossible to concentrate on any mental activity for more
than an hour or two at a time.

The wonder is that he wrote as much as he did. *Among
the Hills* in 1869 was dedicated to Mrs. Fields. *Miriam,* the
story of a dedicated Christian woman married to a pagan
husband, which appeared two years later was inscribed to
Frederick A. P. Barnard, president of Columbia College, in
memory of times when years before in Hartford as young
men they had talked together

> of human life, its hope
> And fear, and unsolved doubts, and what
> It might have been and yet was not

In 1871 he edited the *Journal* of John Woolman and also
helped put together an anthology of poems for children
called *Child-Life,* which was followed two years later by its
sequel, *Child-Life in Prose. The Pennsylvania Pilgrim* in 1872
narrated the achievements of Quaker settlers in "the forest
court of William Penn," and it seemed to Whittier better
than *Snow-Bound.* A collection called *Hazel-Blossoms* appeared in 1875, so named because the "sere and yellow"
witch-hazel leaf reminded Whittier that at sixty-eight his
autumnal muse was withering also. But during the next ten
years five separate volumes appeared; finally, in 1890, not
two years before his death, he issued a valedictory collection
in *At Sundown* which looked backward in reminiscence over
his long career and forward with calm assurance that whatever future waited him was in divine hands—and therefore
good. Whittier might have said of any of these poems of
his last two decades what he said of one of them when he
wrote: "It isn't learned, nor graceful, nor obscure with
transcendentalism—but plain, homely verse as befitted the
subjects and occasion, and I like it, and think others will."[7]

II *A World Too Full*

After 1876, when the marriage of a niece who since the
death of his sister had been his housekeeper at Amesbury

made other arrangements necessary, Whittier moved to the home of cousins at Oak Knoll in Danvers, a rural community not far from Salem, on the old road between Newburyport and Boston. He returned occasionally to Amesbury to vote, visit old friends, and keep his corrective hand in local politics. He went to Boston to sit side by side with old friends Emerson, Longfellow, and Holmes at the famous seventieth birthday dinner in 1877, which is remembered less for Whittier's part in it than for the tremendous *gaffe* which young Samuel Clemens made when he told a funny story about the guests of honor which did not at the time seem funny at all. When Whittier was called on for a speech, he rose, observed one onlooker, "very much abashed, as it was his nature to be. He made a few remarks, saying, 'My voice is of a timorous nature and rarely to be heard above a breath.' "[8]

Whittier was becoming accustomed now to having honors thrust upon him. He had been elected one of the overseers of Harvard in 1858; two years later he had received an honorary master's degree from that institution and in 1886 he was awarded an honorary doctorate. A town in California was named for him, and another college. He was elected to the Authors Club in New York, the Massachusetts Historical Society, the American Philosophical Society, and a Fellow of the American Academy of Arts and Sciences. He never relinquished completely his responsibilities as a leader in Quaker affairs; but, as he grew older, he became less active.

Correspondence and conversations with admirers took much of his time and strength. Everyone knew him, much as everyone today knows Robert Frost; and many came to see him, like pilgrims to a shrine. Many of the visitors were women, and Whittier found many of them delightful. Helen Keller came to see him, and Sarah Orne Jewett. But some were tiresome and broke into his work. "I have had a great many callers," he wrote. "Too many people are constantly coming, and they tire me more than I can well bear." He complained in 1889: "I have been sadly beset with company. Everybody seems after me; the world is too full and is flowing over."[9]

He is said to have spent whole afternoons away from the house to avoid visitors. "I had hard work to lose him, but I've lost him," he would say, "but I never could lose a *her*," especially, he might have added, when she was young and bright and admiring. But for all his protestations, he liked the attention which he received. When at the end of a long afternoon, young visitors, he said, "like birds have flown,"

> I hear their voices, fainter grown,
> And dimly through the dusk I see
> Their kerchiefs wave good-night to me,—
> Light hearts of girlhood, knowing naught
> Of all the cheer their coming brought.

In spite of affectionate ministrations of admirers and friends, Whittier confessed that "at times a great feeling of loneliness comes over me; I miss sadly the dear old faces, and think of days that are no more. My life has not proved," he wrote sadly, "what I dreamed of in youth." Old friends and closest relatives were gone: "only the everlasting beauty of outward Nature remains unchanged." Yet his life seemed incomplete: "I am old enough to be done with work, only that I feel my best words have not been said after all, that what has been said is not its full expression." Longfellow's late poem, "Morituri Salutamus," touched him deeply. "Emerson, Longfellow, Holmes, and myself," he said, "all are getting to be old fellows, and that swan-song might serve us all—'we who are about to die.' God help us all!" Longfellow's death in 1882 saddened him—"There was no blot in the crystal purity of his writings." As for himself, "I do not care for fame," said Whittier, "and have no solicitude for the verdict of posterity." As he thought of himself and of his aging literary friends, he was sure that "What we *are* will then be more important than what we have done or said in prose or rhyme, or what folks that we never saw or heard think of us."[10]

He spent his time quietly at Danvers at his writing desk or beneath surrounding groves of oak and pine and hemlock. As he worked there in 1888 over proofs of the seven-volume collected edition of his prose and verse, he looked with dismay over many of his poems and wished he might drown them "like so many unlikely kittens. But my publishers say there is no getting rid of them, that they have nine lives."[11] Some of the earliest apprentice work was secluded in an appendix, and Whittier did what he could about last-minute improvements of the rest, "correcting a little of the bad grammar and rhythmical blunders which have so long annoyed my friends who have graduated at Harvard instead of a district school."

As time went on, he spent less time at Oak Knoll and more in the Merrimack valley at Amesbury, briefly, or at Newburyport with other cousins with whom he went every summer to one or another of his favorite resorts among the lakes in the foothills of the White Mountains, to the Bearcamp House in West Ossipee, to the Asquam House at Holderness, to Intervale, or to Hampton Falls, where he suffered the paralytic stroke which was harbinger of his death there on September 9, 1892. His body was brought back to Amesbury for a funeral the next day, and Whittier was laid to rest beside his parents and his sister in the old graveyard at Haverhill. His old friend Oliver Wendell Holmes, the last among the veteran voices, remembered him as the "Best loved and saintliest of our singing train" whose "lifelong record closed without a stain, a blameless memory shrined in sacred song."

THE POET

There was ne'er a man born who had more of the swing
Of the true lyric bard and all that kind of thing;
And his failures arise (though he seem not to know it)
From the very cause that has made him a poet,—
A fervor of mind that knows so separation
'Twixt simple excitement and pure inspiration,
                              —JAMES RUSSELL LOWELL

Strictly speaking, Whittier did not care much for literature.
He loved men and things and books of biography and travel;
he liked to know how the world looked and what brave
spirits had wrought it.
                              —NATHANIEL HAWTHORNE

Art should be independent of . . . devotion, pity, love,
patriotism, and the like.
                              —JAMES MCNEILL WHISTLER

The Beauty of Holiness

I love the old melodious lays
Which softly melt the ages through,
The songs of Spenser's golden days,
Arcadian Sidney's silvery phrase,
Sprinkling our noon of time with freshest
morning dew.

Yet, vainly in my quiet hours
To breathe their marvelous notes I try;
I feel them, as the leaves and flowers
In silence feel the dewy showers,
And drink with glad, still lips the blessing
of the sky.

—"Proem"

THE FIRST THING to say about Whittier as a poet is that he was candid in recognizing his limitations. The next is to suggest that, considering his time and place and his background and opportunities for learning, Whittier was probably as good a poet as he could have been. Another way of expressing much the same thought would be to say that he was as good a poet as he deserved to be or as his countrymen deserved to have. His persistent belittling of his own verse was more than an expression of Quaker humility or rustic modesty. When he spoke in "Proem" of the "rigor of a frozen clime" and the "harshness of an untaught ear" as obstacles in his way, he spoke with a poet's insight of profound deficiencies in himself and among the people who read him. "I am not a builder in the sense of Milton's phrase of one who could 'build the lofty rhyme,'" he said. "My vehicles have been of the humbler sort—merely the farm wagons and buckboards of verse." They were not so well constructed, he thought, as Holmes's "One Hoss Shay"; and they could not, like that fabled vehicle, last one hundred years: "I should not dare to warrant any of my work for a long drive."[1]

Yet now, when almost a century has passed since Whittier's better verse was written, it gives little indication of being ready to fall to pieces all at once. Or, if it has fallen or is about to fall, fragments may be found among the wreckage. Some are only shreds and tatters of rhyme, like

> "Shoot, if you must, this old grey head,
> "But spare your country's flag," she said,

or an opening couplet which contains more sentimental suggestion than the lines which follow it,

> Blessings on thee, little man,
> Barefoot boy with cheek of tan,

or an occasional quatrain which flashes out from among its torpid companions, like

> "I'm sorry that I spelt the word;
> "I hate to go above you
> "Because,"—the brown eyes lower fell,—
> "Because, you see, I love you."

or moralistic tags worn smooth by repetition, like

> Of all sad words of tongue or pen
> The saddest are, "It might have been."

These are among the ingredients of household verse, and Whittier mixed them well enough to satisfy popular palates. Not even Longfellow, Holmes, nor James Whitcomb Riley was a more expert short-order cook in literature. Simply prepared according to familiar recipes, with small attention to subtleties of flavor, the product was meant for quick consumption by busy people who must eat and run. Because easily digested, it produced no rumblings to disturb a countryman's placid concern with matters of more worldly interest. Whatever its vitamin deficiency, it was nourishing enough to carry him over until he next required brief refreshment. Most important, it was what he was used to—and liked best.

I *The Reason and the Purpose*

Whittier aspired to better achievement. In some of his earliest prose, when at twenty-two he was editor of the *American Manufacturer,* he complained that American writers lacked "the sternness of thought—the concentrated power— the overmastering grasp of imagination" necessary for successful composition. He spoke of the "imbecility" of native poetry, which failed in strength and boldness, which was satisfied with "light flashes of fancy—the tinsel and drapery of poetry." The verse which his contemporaries produced was "pleasant and familiar, and not infrequently beautiful"; but it skimmed along surfaces without "manly vigorous exertion," with "no character of thought—no deep, engrossing interest to chain down our sympathies and work upon the sterner passions." Yet why, he asked, should any American poet "quit his fanciful and flowery path for a darker and ruder pilgrimage? Why exchange his easy and popular style, to make exhausting and' uncertain effort for something more substantial and elevated?" He would thus deprive himself of readers: "Why shut himself from the world, and sacrifice the body to the workings of the soul, for that fame which is seldom awarded to true genius until the wearied spirit has gone to its last and wakeless slumber."[2]

These sentences are surely ironical, the quizzically distorted reflections of a Quaker who knows deep within him that applause of worldly men does not measure success. They represent also the attitude of a prudent New England countryman who knows through experience that the world is much with him and that its requirements must be met. The indictment which Whittier so early made against young America was not new; for Philip Freneau, then in retirement at his New Jersey farm, had made much the same charge thirty years before when he had attacked the sentimentality of poetasters of his day. In the intervening years other voices had spoken, less loudly and with less professional assurance. What distinguishes Whittier's young utterance is that it is the first strong public statement by one of his literary generation of attitudes which ten years later Edgar Allan Poe was to extend with more effective emphasis.

In the *New England Weekly Review* of August 9, 1830, Whittier again attacked "our love-sick and moon-struck rhymers," the dandies of literature: "We are weary—disgusted —and ill-natured in contempation of . . . this eternal rhyming to cheek and eye and headgear—this mawkish affectation of sentiment—this profanation of the purity and holiness of love." Such verse was "enough to drive one . . . into absolute madness." Part of the trouble, he thought, as Charles Brock-den Brown had three decades before, was a lack of honest and informed criticism among his countrymen. "Most of our literary periodicals are too timid, in fact too dependent, to give their opinions with the firmness and regard for truth which are necessary." He was not only speaking of the New England in which, Emerson was to charge, there had been no new thought since the turn of the century; for Whittier early had his critical eye on a larger audience—the nation. The strength of the old generation of Jefferson and Adams was gone; and in its place softness spread over the land, an inclination to compromise with old ideals. "We are becoming effeminate," said Whittier, "in everything—in our habits as well as our literature, and there is no one fearless enough to investigate the causes of our weakness and apply the requisite remedies."[3]

James Gates Percival, the New England poet who went mad, his friends thought, because he had read too much Byron, seemed to Whittier an exception. He "went forth in the dignity and power of man—to grapple with the dark thoughts which thronged before him, molding them into visible and tangible realities."[4] John G. C. Brainard, formerly of Hartford, had been another. Though unpolished, his verses reflected something of the spirit of old English balladry, without the licentiousness of Byron or Shelley or Thomas Moore; and they were wholly American: "He prefers the lowliest blossom of Yankeeland to the gorgeous magnolia and the orange bower of another clime." Like the gifted but unfortunate Burns, Brainard's strong, untutored mind was bold, vigorous, eloquent, powerful, and his verse was a model for native poets.

Meanwhile Whittier fumbled to find his own voice, his own words. He has too often been facilely labeled as an "American Burns" because, untutored, he sang of native scene and country people—and as if the influence of the Scottish poet were unique upon him. Burns was one among a dozen poets with whose tone and rhythms young Whittier practiced. His taste was not always good; his judgments were often prejudiced. He read and dismissed most of the prominent English romantics. He was early attracted to Byron's verse, delighting like many of his generation in its vigorous unrestraint; but he was repelled by what he knew of Byron's life. Like Shelley—of whose "enchanting productions," Whittier confessed, "none could be more enthusiastically fond"— Byron spoiled fine poetry with licentiousness: "mere Genius shall never take precedence of Virtue." And "even the gifted Shelley wearies us with his sickly conceits and unsubstantial themes." Whittier admired Scott, especially "the magnificence of his prose" which "eclipsed the temporary splendor of his poetry." Southey seemed wildly ridiculous; Wordsworth, "with all his fine perceptions of natural beauty, and his exquisite philosophy, sinks at times into the most disgusting puerility— the pathos and sentimentality of an overgrown baby"; and Keats's "Endymion" was mawkish and affected. Elizabeth Barrett was admired because she was bravely an invalid; and Alexander Pushkin was praised because he proved that Negro blood did not deprive a man of genius.[5]

What can be said for such a man? He threw Whitman's *Leaves of Grass* into the fire in disgust. He had no taste for Poe, thought Thoreau wicked, and seems to have been unaware of Melville. Paul Elmer More was correct when he observed that what Whittier needed more than anything else was "a canon of taste, which might have driven him to stiffen his work, to purge away the flaccid and set the occasionally achieved genuine poetry in stronger relief."[6] Among his contemporaries, besides Percival and Brainard, he early admired Lydia Sigourney, the sweet singer of Hartford; later, the thin-strung verse of Alice and Phoebe Carey; and the pathos of Grace Greenwood and Mrs. E. D. E. N. Southworth. Hawthorne struck him as a pretty writer, proficient in much the manner of Hans Christian Andersen. The perfect novelist, he thought, would be a combination of Brockden Brown and Fenimore Cooper. Longfellow's "The Psalm of Life" was to seem "worth more than all the dreams of Shelley, Keats, and Wordsworth": There was "no blot on the crystal purity of his writings."[7]

Except in his admiration for Coleridge and Milton—for their freedom-loving prose rather than for their poetry—and his conventional lip service to Shakespeare, Spenser, and Marvell, Whittier was almost always wrong in his estimate of other men's writings. As he looked back late in life, he saw that his century had been prolific in song, especially in the United States. He would blame no man, he said, who esteemed Emerson's "Threnody" as better than Milton's "Lycidas." He rejoiced in the sweet morality of Longfellow, whose pleasant lines helped shape "the present culture of our English-speaking people at home and abroad." Close to the summit of American achievement, notable for "truth and nature, wit and wisdom," rested Bryant's "Robert of Lincoln," Emerson's "Humblebee," Lowell's "Courtin'," and Whittier's consistent favorite, Dr. Holmes's "The Deacon's Masterpiece," which he and all his friends referred to as the "One-Hoss Shay."[8]

To suggest that Whittier was deficient in literary judgment is not enough. Better poets than he have mistaken their contemporaries. Nor is his conception of the function of poetry solely to blame. Though poets have used other terms to describe it, many, perhaps most of them, have thought of their lines not only as quick-probing insights toward truth and explanatory of the ways of God to man but also as precautionary or corrective—as warnings to man of ways he must not go. When Whittier playfully accused himself in "The Tent on the Beach,"

> You check the free play of your rhymes to clap
> A moral underneath, and spring it like a trap,

he was speaking only of lack of subtlety in execution. He had learned from Milton that great poetry required moral purpose and that it reflected the morality of the poet.

He learned, that is, what Milton said about poetry; what he had little opportunity to learn was how superior poetry was made. He lacked that aesthetic education which might have provided the literary counterbalance to the moralist in him. No poem is in any way better or wiser or more penetrating than the poet who created it at his greatest stretch can be. Perhaps, therefore, the simplest way of expressing Whittier's limitation is to say that he did not know enough. The makers of verse against whom he matched his early talent created the patterns, in metrics and content, from which he was never successfully to escape. The simple ballad stanzas of Burns, the loosely bound narrative patterns of Scott and Byron, the faithful search for native themes suggested by the untaught Brainard, and the simple, superficial morality admired in the popular verse of Mrs. Sigourney and Felicia Hemans fitted Whittier finally to a mold from which he seldom ever broke. In "Proem," he was to recognize his lack of "rounded art" and to think that it was his "unanointed eyes" and lack of "seer-like power" which deprived him of ability

> to show
> The secrets of the heart and mind;
> To drop the plummet-line below
> Our common world of joy and woe,
> A more intense despair or higher hope to find.

His words give him away. Accepting contemporary notions that poetry was "rather an *Art* than a *Science*," that the "divine creative faculty" insured "energy, enthusiasm, beauty, abandonment to the emotions, and . . . spontaneous adaptation of language and rhythm to their subjects," he was yet unable to go all the way with Emerson in recognizing, not meter, but meter-making thought as an essential of poetry. Whittier objected to imperfect rhyming or verse without the smoothness of regularity; to him irregular odes made music "about as pleasing to the ear as that of a Sawmill or a Steam engine."[9]

He loved best "the old melodious lays" sung in simple rhythms. A straightforward iambic measure, four beats to the line, precisely measured out with rhyme, or ruminative and pictorial blank verse such as Wordsworth did much better, most often served Whittier to express his earnest sense of human rights or to reproduce what he described in "The Tent on the Beach" as "Such music as the woods and streams Sang in his ear."

Newspaper verse of his time probably directed Whittier to the forms, rhythms, and measures which he most frequently used. About one-third of his poems were written in four-stress lines, ordinarily in octosyllabic couplets. About one-fourth were in ballad measure, alternating lines of four and three stress. He seldom attempted complicated stanzaic forms; he never, for example, wrote a sonnet. The simpler the pattern, the better. Old thoughts required old forms, and Whittier seems seldom to have groped—as Emerson, Whitman, or Tennyson did—to discover poetic techniques which would add dimensions to his meaning. He preferred, he said, in "The Peace,"

To paint, forgetful of the tricks of art,
  With pencil dipped alone in colors of the heart.

How expertly one can paint with a pencil, no matter how bright the colors into which it is dipped, is perhaps to be questioned. Whittier allowed himself little time to consider niceties of that kind. But to attempt a poem, he once said, without being "consecrated to the sacred interests of religion and humanity would be a criminal waste of life." Matters of form or method were less important. Nature herself was a tangle of mixed, apparently inappropriate, metaphors. Literary style could be corrected by editors or improved by admiring friends. Whittier's grateful use of other people's suggestions about words or phrases he should have used identifies him as a humble man, but not as an artist.

What Whittier did not know, or knew too late, when the pattern of his writing was set, was the power and beauty and intricacy which provide essential resilience to great poetry. He bought Shakespeare early, when as a boy he visited relatives in Boston, but his verse at that time or later provides little evidence that he read him with more than casually admiring attention. He received from Shakespeare what he was prepared to receive—a handful of quotations or allusions, and the discovery that Shakespeare was also fond of picturing village people and ghostly spirits. Whittier's acquaintance with poetry was that of an avid schoolboy until he was almost thirty; he read widely but without direction in whatever volumes came to hand. The literature of classic Greece came to him in "mirth-provoking" versions told about the kitchen fire by one of the few college graduates young Whittier knew, his Dartmouth-trained schoolmaster who so mixed Yankee whimsicality with ancient lore that Olympus seemed a local huckleberry hill. If an older Whittier ever read Homer or Aeschylus, he read as men of settled mind will read: to discover illustrations or approval of what he already knew. He was to recommend Boccaccio and Goethe and Jean Paul because of their talent for portraying innocently beautiful children.

Like Whitman and Melville and Mark Twain, Whittier was self-taught in literature. He shared with them—and with Hart Crane, Robert Frost, and perhaps all poets anywhere —the advantages and encumbrances of feeling with strength beyond his power to record. Each would subscribe, with personal reservations, to the perhaps irrefutable notion that poets are born, not made—a conception which is perhaps exceptionally persuasive in a democracy, for sometimes it may be supposed even unpatriotic to consider any other. Among the inalienable rights is that which allows any man to speak; and when he speaks rudely well, without bothering with traditional trickeries of art, his lack of artistry is a kind of confirmation of convictions about one person being as good as any other. Too much nicety is neither appropriate nor manly.

Literature in the United States is different from literature in many other places because of the kind of preparation its best writers have had for producing it. Until T. S. Eliot and Ezra Pound spoiled the scheme, it was possible to explain that after Thoreau graduated from Harvard in 1837 no major American writer had completed formal collegiate training. Like Whittier or Whitman, William Dean Howells, and Mark Twain, they came to literature through popular journalism. Or, like Melville and Henry James, they hungrily followed whatever directions were open to them in acquiring foundations upon which their talents might build. It is not necessary because of this to suppose that collegiate education is a bad thing because so many men have succeeded so well without it, or that it is essential preparation for men of letters and that writers in the United States would have been better if they had had it—though either possibility may be argued. What can be recognized is that successful writing in the kind of democracy which has developed in the United States will inevitably, as de Tocqueville was the first to explain, take directions of its own.

It will be democratic and romantic, which two words so overlap in meaning that they may be nearly synonymous. It will be simple: it will be direct and to the point, without flimflammery of decoration which is unmanly or unpleasing either to simple men or in the eyes of a God who has provided in nature and in the dedicated human spirit efficient beauties sufficient for the satisfaction of man. It will express what each man knows through his own observation, and it will be persuasively addressed to the understanding of all men. Because man is the image of God and all nature images His handiwork, it will translate mundane fact to spiritual truth and say, for example, that man in his weakness is sustained by the everlasting arms of God, knowing that God really has no arms in the pictorial sense in which they are here spoken of, but that the image is as close as most men can come to expressing or understanding the comfort of belief.

This literature will become, as Emerson and Thoreau made it, a literature of symbols; a literature fond of meaning more than it says; a literature, said D. H. Lawrence, which will not take its clothes off, so that Melville, for one, can reveal his questing quarrel through the attractive device of a voyage at sea. Charles Feidelson has spoken instructively of these things in his survey of *Symbolism and American Literature*. Richard Chase in *American Literature and Its Tradition* has pointed to distinguishing directions in native fiction. R. W. B. Lewis in *The American Adam* underlines the restless search for discovery of radical virtues like those of man before he was expelled from Paradise. In the freedom of opportunity in a new world each man might become whatever his talents would allow him; old ways of being could be thrust aside. John Kouwenhoven has suggested that Americans are known, in literature and almost everything else, for interest in process rather than product, in becoming rather than being, in getting about rather than standing still. Tales of voyaging like *Moby Dick* or *The Adventures of Huckleberry Finn*, which within their forms seem formless as if the questing might go on forever, seem distinctively American. So do chewing gum and soap operas, skyscrapers, and jazz.

Observations like these are important aids to understanding America's still-restless quest for self-discovery. From Jonathan Edwards to Lionel Trilling, from Hawthorne to Faulkner, from Whitman to T. S. Eliot, effective literary voices among us have been raised to explain where we *should* or *might* or *must* be going. When they have searched the past, it has been to measure the future. Like Emerson and Melville, they have recognized the present, its necessity for compromise and hardship and sin; but the present has been the spot where man stands on a moving belt which propels him toward something beyond. Long before America was known, many people had thought that this is what superior literature should do: guide and inspire.

But there is another kind of writing, not altogether different, except in emphasis. It will look backward, even with satisfaction, on where man has been. Or it will pause to look around to notice where man stands now. As a creature of his time, Whittier shared most of the forward-looking characteristics of his contemporaries; there was not among them a more directing or corrective writer. Anticipating Hawthorne, Longfellow, and Francis Parkman in their retrospective moods, he differed from them by searching through the American past to discover in history or in familiar lore examples of ancestral virtues in which his countrymen might take pride. He paused also to gaze with appreciative wonder at the hills and streams and farmlands of New England, bathed in beauties which could make man glad. He lingered over little things, like the swarming of bees or the raking of hay, to present what he called Flemish pictures of simple life. Like William Dean Howells and Robert Frost he confronted the commonplace to reveal the uncomplicated satisfactions of unimportant people who were brave or strong or erring—but always human.

At forty, when his reputation was beginning to be established, Whittier lamented that "poetry of Home, of Nature, of the Affections . . . is sadly wanting in our young literature." America had, he said, no native pastorals, no balladry, no simple songs to remind her people that men and women much like themselves had met, loved, and parted, and that the tragedy and comedy of life had been endlessly enacted in local settings. "Poetry is not one of our household gods," he said. "Our poetry is cold—abstract—imitation—the labor of overtasked and jaded intellectuals, rather than the spontaneous outgushing of hearts warm with love, and sympathizing with human nature as it actually exists about us—with the joys and griefs, the good and even the ill of our common humanity."[10]

Whittier wrote as he wrote because he wanted to write that way. "What I had," he said in "The Panorama," "I gave." He knew himself a minor poet, humbly offering his mite, but at the same shrine at which greater poets worshiped. To say this is more than to say that he meant well. Almost every writer does that. The critical task is to discover, not what he intended nor how good a man he was, not even to underline his physical deficiencies like color blindness and tone deafness and susceptibility to weariness, nor to approve his pristine depths of spiritual commitment. These are of the man, who is in almost every respect admirable, and who as a man deserves the veneration which generations of admirers have given him. The task is to look again at what he wrote, lest all be discarded because much is bad.

II *The Emphatic Poet*

His kind of poetry, Hyatt Waggoner reminds us, "is almost the exact counterpart of what the modern poets have taught us to like and think of as good. If James's idea that what is stated is not literature and what is literature is not stated is the whole truth, then most of Whittier's is not literature. It states emphatically. It aims to convey truth and influence moral attitudes. It is relaxed, ruminative, placid, unambiguous, 'thin.'" Few readers need read Whittier twice to comprehend his meaning; yet many, in his time and ours, reread him for the pleasure of discovering familiar words well spoken. "Only if we can bring ourselves to grant," continues Mr. Waggoner, "that a lack of irony, ambiguity, and other hallmarks of the modern mind, and a fondness for plain statement, are not necessarily fatal to poetry, can we attain a position from which it is possible to make even a limited claim for Whittier as a poet."[11]

Walt Whitman found Whittier "pretty lean and ascetic." He was "not composite and universal enough (doesn't like to be, doesn't try to be) for ideal Americanism." His morality seemed incomplete, strained through Puritan and Quaker filters, but as such was "very valuable as genuine utterance." Though "unmistakably hued with zealous partisan anti-slavery coloring," his genre pieces of local Yankee life seemed gloriously good to Whitman. In all, Whittier struck him as "rather a grand figure." To Lowell who knew him better but perhaps judged less well, he seemed "the most representative poet that New England has produced," singing her thoughts, prejudices, and scenery: "Whatever Mr. Whittier may lack, he has the prime merit that he smacks of the soil."[12] His words were attached to things as much perhaps as those of any of his contemporaries except Emily Dickinson, who sang unheard, and Walt Whitman, who often shouted so loudly that he was misunderstood.

Time sorts the work of any writer, ignoring what is drab, preserving what has possibility for continuing life. Many of the unmistakably excellent, like Donne or Coleridge, Keats or Poe, are left with a residue which fills only a slender volume. Whittier discarded much when he put together the four volumes of his *Complete Poems,* and he says he would have discarded more if his publisher had not objected. He divided his verse then into eight kinds, and he exercised what may be considered a mature and retrospective judgment of their ascending order of worthiness. They were placed into two groups: first, the "Narrative and Legendary Poems,"

"Poems of Nature," "Personal Poems," and "Occasional Poems," followed as if in summary by "The Tent on the Beach," which encompasses all of these kinds and looks toward the second grouping of "Anti-Slavery Poems," "Poems of Labor and Reform," "Poems Subjective and Reminiscent," and "Religious Poems," these capped by the valedictory "At Sundown." As if embarrassed to be included in the company of better poems, a careful selection of early and uncollected verses appeared in smaller print as an appendix.

Any poet's estimate of his product, even his grouping of it, is instructive to the critical reader; but it does only part of his work. Whittier's writing is not of so many kinds as his arrangement of it suggests. His religious convictions and his delight in nature have been seen to color virtually all his writing. They represent his most deeply cherished beliefs and his most ardent response to their verification in the world around him. When either appears alone in his verses, unsupported by the other, the result is sometimes briefly charming or inspirational; but they do not often appear alone. Love of God and admiration of God's handiwork, two aspects of a single view, are hallmarks which distinguish Whittier as a good man; and they infiltrate to all of his writing which is best, whether in poems of persuasion, in the recreation of time past, or in reminiscence of experiences which have brought him peace.

Nature to him was various, and often best when somewhat wild. He speaks of the "picturesque inequality of Nature" which "eschews regular outlines." She does not "work with square and compass, or lay on her colors by the rules of royal artists or the dunces of the academies." Whittier admired "her primitive woods; scattered trees, with moist sward and bright mosses at their roots; great clumps of green shadow, where limb intwists with limb and the rustle of one leaf stirs a hundred others,—stretching up steep hillsides, flooding with green beauty the valleys, or arching over with leaves the sharp ravines, every tree and shrub unlike its neighbor in size and proportion,—the old and storm-broken leaning on the young and vigorous—intricate and confused, without order or method." What man would exchange this natural scene, he asked, "for artificial French gardens, where every tree stands stiff and regular, clipped and trimmed into unvarying conformity."[13]

Whittier speaks here as most men of his time spoke. The complex and charming disarray of nature—her confusion of cloud and sunlight, her exuberant embrace of foul with fair—testified to a magnificence which shrugged away the disfiguring garments of form in which men would clothe her. She was to be accepted for what she was: the reflection of a plan larger than any man's ability to explain. She was the captivating, mute ambassador of "life, light, beauty everywhere," who spoke in gestures which pointed toward truths of greater beauty and eternal goodness.

Whittier never doubted that behind the disheveled countenance of nature and the "maddening maze of human suffering and greed" shone the light of divine beneficence: "Surely God would not permit his children to suffer if it were not to work out for them the highest good. For God never does, nor suffers to be done, but that which we would do if we could see the end of all events as well as He." Who then was man to doubt the wisdom or the harmonious beauty of God's ways? "God's love is so infinitely greater than mine that I cannot fear for his children, and when I long to help some poor suffering, erring fellow-creature, I am consoled with the thought that His great heart of love is more than mine can be, and so I rest in peace."[14]

Whittier did not easily square his sense of the beauty of external nature with his early Quaker training which warned that love of sensuous beauty was a lure which could tempt man from recognition of higher, spiritual beauties. He spoke of the "charming spell" which beauty cast on him, and of himself as "beauty's powerless slave." His disposition, he said, was naturally "ardent, impetuous, imaginative, powerfully acted upon from without, keenly susceptible to all influences." Beauty, however, was more than tinsel; it was more than a magnificent sunset or a broad green vista of hill and valley or the tantalizing grace of a lovely girl. It was these things, or in these things, but it was also more than these. Even in his earliest writings, Whittier spoke of the beauty of "a spirit of a higher mould, A being unallied to earth," of beauty that was a "stainless . . . veiled and holy shrine." Later he spoke of the "unsung beauty" hidden in common things, beauty in self-discipline and labor: "beauty made the bride of use," walking "hand in hand with duty." Speaking of the Puritans, "strongly faithful to duty, in peril and suffering and self-denial," he declared: "They lived a truer poetry than Homer or Virgil wrote." For beauty was goodness, and beauty was truth. It existed not in the object, but in the eye of the beholder.[15]

True beauty was "the beauty of holiness, of purity, of that inward grace which passeth show." It was not line or form, proportion or coloring, not chiseled from marble nor wrought on canvas: "The heart feels a beauty of another kind; looking through the outward environment, it discovers a deeper and more real loveliness." Beauty like this was to be found everywhere, in common things made radiant because of their relation to an eternal, harmonious scheme which was supernal beauty. The truth and beauty and goodness of God were one, and beauty could not be apprehended without recognition at the same time of truth and goodness. With Keats, and almost any other of his time, Whittier was sure that that was all he needed to know. He would not have agreed with Poe, who said much the same thing, but with different emphasis; who explained that the poet's projectile aimed toward beauty would never hit its mark if burdened with the weight of instruction or morality, but that, unencumbered, it might streak toward beauty and, if successful in arriving there, would then discover truth and goodness by its side.

In Poe's terms, Whittier was not satisfied with simply being a poet. He failed to recognize the limitations or the possibilities of his art. Inspired but confused by notions shared with many of his time about the responsibility of the artist toward bettering his fellow men and glorifying God, he was diverted from the proper business of the poet, which is to write honestly and well. The artist's honesty, it might be said, is not tested by allegiance to creed or attitude toward the welfare of his fellows, but by the freshness and rightness of his perception. His talents are put inadequately to use when they serve only as buttresses to what already exists. If that is a kind of art, it is not in a true sense creative, but re-creative; it is similar to that of the copyist in painting or the instrumentalist in music who reproduces, with however superb a skill, what has been done perhaps as well before. Much that Whittier wrote was an underlining or intensification of wonderfully compelling aspirations common to all men. At his best, he reminded them of duty, of the necessity for love, and of the benison of beauty. It may be that rousing men or lulling them to quietness and peace is a good, even a necessary occupation. But most poets have aimed at something more.

Emerson once suggested that the purpose of any writer who spoke directly to the spirit was not to comfort or to settle anything. His aim, he said, was to unsettle all things. It is not necessary to agree with William Carlos Williams' pert suggestion that "Of sugar and spice and all things nice, That is what bad poetry is made of"; but it is possible to wonder why so little important poetry has ever been explicitly religious. Both born of the spirit of man, religion and poetry seem inevitably related. Almost every person who thinks seriously about either attempts at one time or another to explain their relationship or to distinguish between them. Each reaches or has reached beyond things as they appear to be toward suggestions or affirmations of what they really are. One difference may be that poetry reaches while religion has reached, that one is a continuing revelation and the other the remembrance of precedent revelation.

The symbols and traditional rubrics of religion, perhaps because they are worn by time, have often proved an encumbrance to the poet. It is possible to say that true religion, stripped of retrospective veneration of ritual or creed, and true poetry are the same, or that the poet is the most religious because the most revealing of men, and that the truly religious man is always a poet. Whatever the intimations of truth hidden behind phrases like these, their demonstration requires more subtle explanation than any but the best poets bring forth. What does seem plain is that what is ordinarily thought of as religion has not often fitted successfully into what most people think of as the best poetry.

To say that Whittier's religion colored everything he wrote is to say of him no more or no less than can be said of Dante, Milton, T. S. Eliot, or the clergyman in the church down any street. Each, in his own terms, attempts to justify the ways of God to man. Dante, Milton, and Eliot have usually done it as poets do—by creating forms which not only contain all which can be expressed of their insight or belief but also reach beyond that to suggest what cannot be verbalized. The clergyman may or may not be a poet. The chances are that he effectively influences his listeners to recognition of moral and spiritual virtues which tradition and daily experience certify as good for man. He may well speak of the inexpressible beauty of holiness, of comfort within the everlasting arms, and of truths revealed by the voice within. He will point to analogies between stories from scripture and the everyday life of men. He will use familiar rhetorical devices—God is like a father—to comfort or inspire. His purpose is to help and direct his congregation—he, the shepherd; they, his flock. He is a dedicated man, good in every common sense, and willing to sacrifice much of himself in the hope of salvation for others.

Whittier was like that. "Dear Lord and Father of Mankind," he prayed, "Forgive our foolish ways." Generations of worshipful Christians have been moved by the transparent sincerity of his hymns, so simply devout, unspoiled by intricacies of theology or niceties of denominational creed. The Methodist Hymnal contains more hymns by Whittier than by any other writer except Isaac Watts and Charles Wesley. More than seventy hymns now in use were written by him. When sixty-five hymns were chosen by an interdenominational Congress of Religion in Chicago in 1893, nine were by the Quaker poet—in the meetinghouses of whose faith no hymns were sung. Presbyterians, Baptists, Congregationalists—all who sing joyful or reverential praises to the Lord—respond to his call to "Follow with reverent steps the great example of Him whose holy work was doing good," so that "Each loving life" may be "a psalm of gratitude." He has helped them remember that there is an "Immortal Love, forever full, Forever flowing free, Forever shared, forever whole, A never ebbing sea."

Because Whittier thus sang close to the hearts of so many people who, like him, have wished no greater joy than devout resignation of their lives to a strength much beyond their own, it is not likely that he will be forgotten. He receives and he deserves continuing gratitude for the solace he provides and for the challenge which he offers those who join him in quiet aspiration. Few better men have ever written, or few braver men more sincerely committed. His rhymes have struck responsive echoes in the hearts of many fine men and women, and he has appealed to children also. But that is not to say that he was always a poet.

CHAPTER 6

Words as Weapons

Yet here, at least an earnest sense
Of human right and weal is shown;
A hate of tyranny intense,
And hearty in its vehemence,
As if my brother's pain and sorrow were my own.

O freedom! if to me belong
No mighty Milton's gift divine,
Nor Marvell's wit and graceful song,
Still with a love as deep and strong
As theirs, I lay, like them, my best gifts on thy shrine.
                                        —"Proem"

IN SPEAKING of Hawthorne and Melville, one is likely to emphasize their concern with the conflict in man between the head and the heart. In considering Emerson, it is important to recognize the difference between what he meant by understanding, which represents man's logical, rational, constructive faculties, and what he meant by reason, which is man's ability intuitively to apprehend truths revealed by the divine spirit within him. Emerson, like Melville and Hawthorne, was enough a man of the world to know that life could not be successfully lived without attention to necessities controlled by the understanding. He saw that man must manage to live with equal attention given to what he might be and what he must be.

I *The Quiet Voice*

The difference between Whittier and these men was a matter of degree, for they shared fundamental assumptions of their age. Each was sure of man's infinite capacity to be better than man usually was. Transcending his ability to think through to truth was his capacity to apprehend truth without the intervention of thought. All that stood between man and immediate revelation was his humanity. Crippled by what, for lack of a better word, was called *sin,* his thinking was distorted by prejudice or disturbed by pride. Even the state of his physical health influenced it, though sometimes illness provided a shelter from the world or a quiet garden which opened on vistas other men could not see. Thought supplied a light too faint to penetrate deeply into important mysteries. Yet one did not sit in Yogi stillness, waiting the brighter gleam of inner light. Life called also for action, participation, for being up and doing. However Whitman might talk of loafing and inviting his soul or Emerson might boast of becoming a transparent eyeball which in seeing knew all, most men set out, patiently like Thoreau or desperately like Melville, in active pursuit of truths beyond the reach of understanding.

Whittier's vision was clearer because simpler than that of most of his contemporaries. As a Quaker, he knew the immediate power of the still, small voice. It was a quiet voice, not often thundering in wrath or scornful in recrimination; and one had to be quiet to hear it. Excitement, anger, or fervid expectation were to be avoided because the pounding of one's blood might be mistaken for the voice of God. Ritual could not coerce it, nor could other men spell out its message. It was personal. Not Pope nor priest nor elder could give ransom, said Whittier, for the soul of another. The voice spoke directly to each person, yet each person hearing it knew that it spoke the same words incessantly to all persons— but all persons were not often still enough to listen. Whittier knew as well as Emerson that what was true for him in his own heart was true for all men.

He who could hear bore responsibilities for passing on these truths to other men who heard less clearly. He became, if not his brother's keeper, his conscience and his guide. He was motivated by what might be called the higher egotism. Among less dedicated people such attitudes were likely to breed arrogance or pride: Hawthorne spoke of them in "Ethan Brand" and Melville's Captain Ahab explains many of their tragic consequences. Except in a radical sense Whittier was the least vainglorious of men. Humbly and with reverence, but with confidence also that the inner voice comprehended all truth, he made himself an instrument which recorded and then played back what had been spoken to him. He called his skill at making verses a wretched talent; but it finally seemed his single gift, which he shared happily, asking his countrymen in "The Panorama" to

> Forget the poet, but his warning heed,
> And shame his poor word with your nobler deed.

What Whittier spoke of was not a matter for thought: it was for feeling; for admiration, awe, gratitude; for pity for the suffering; for anger at the unrighteous. He rarely revealed anything of his own religious experiences or personal sources of inspiration. Revelation seems not to have come to him in single, blinding flashes. His verse contains no hint of epiphanies, of mystic moments when all was suddenly made clear. The plain truth and piety of which he did speak were those which he had always known and which all men could know. His was an expression, it has been said, of the Christian conscience at its purest and best. Many of his poems are simple exhortations to faith in divine goodness and in the promise of goodness in man. He set forth the most radical of Christian ordinances: Let us therefore love one another.

To Whittier, failure in love set the world askew. What places his writings about reform apart from those of others of his time who would reconstruct mankind according to some exemplary plan is that his was so profoundly simple. "If all the reformers of his age had had Whittier's humility and his faith and vision," Hyatt Waggoner has suggested, "Hawthorne might not have been moved to satirize reformism in *The Blithedale Romance* or James in *The Bostonians*. Whittier's anti-slavery poems are not irrelevant to us because legal slavery no longer exists, nor is their relevance simply a function of the fact that the fight for justice and brotherhood is never ended. The poems . . . are not propaganda verse so much as they are visions of a great society, the City of God on earth, and denunciations of all that hinders its arrival."[1]

II *God and Democracy*

The City of God would inevitably be inhabited by free American democrats, "striving openly and honestly to practice the great truths which lie at the foundation of our republic: all men created equal, endowed with rights inalienable." But it is a mistake to think of Whittier's antislavery activities as a result of his political notions, for to him slavery was more than a social or an economic evil. Not only was it contrary to the most cherished of human values, it was also blasphemy. "Slavery is, in fact, a struggle with the Almighty for dominion over His rational creatures. It is leagued with the powers of darkness, in wresting man from his maker. . . . The voice of God condemns it in the deep places of the human heart."

Anger filled the gentle Whittier at the thought that any man would dare attempt to dehumanize another: treat him as animals are treated, rob him of moral agency, buy and sell him for earthly profit. Whittier did not feel sympathy for the slave solely because he was a suffering man: he was a being tenanted with an immortal soul which no man, not even himself, could own. "All souls are mine," God said. How abysmally improper then it seemed that some men should arrogate to themselves the right to change God's wondrously harmonious plan! "The woes and wrongs unutterable," said Whittier, "which attend this dreadful violation of natural justice, the stripes, the tortures, the sunderings of kindred, the desolation of human affections, the unchastity and lust, the toil uncompensated, the abrogated marriage, the legalized heathenism, the burial of mind, are but incidents to the first grand outrage, that seizure of the entire man, nerve, sinew, and spirit, which robs him of his body, and God of his soul."

Greatly more than an imposition on man, slavery was thus an impious insult to the majesty of God. As a man, Whittier always suffered with the suffering—his family, his friends, his neighbors, people anywhere. Suffering was one of the things which man did not understand. It was to be accepted as part of God's incomprehensible plan. It could sometimes be a blessing, people said, in disguise: a person could be "taught by suffering." But when men deliberately imposed suffering in opposition to what had been revealed as the will of God, then must all other men of good faith join to oppose them. The preservation of what God had made was a sacred duty. "Let us work, then," said Whittier of slavery, "to hasten its downfall, doing whatsoever our hands find to do, with all our might."

Democracy, society, health, fame—these stood in line behind and dependent upon Whittier's simply devout allegiance to what he was certain was God's will. He sympathized with the schemes of political and social theorists of his day: "it becomes us," he said, "to look kindly upon all attempts to apply those doctrines to the details of human life." But in the better doctrine of Christianity, he asserted, "alone rests our hope for humanity." If Whittier—mistaking, as Lowell said, excitement for inspiration—was sometimes shrill, he seldom allowed even his outraged anger to distort this vision. "As honest men," he said, "we needs must act; let us do so as becomes men engaged in a great and solemn cause." To present the misery and degradation of slavery in its simplest, human terms was enough; truth would then inevitably penetrate to the hearts of all men. "We need no disguises, nor false pretenses, nor subterfuges; enough for us to present before our fellow-countrymen the holy truths of freedom in their unadorned and native beauty."[2]

What the head could not understand, the heart could know. Whittier himself was not eminently an intellectual man; but he would be hurt to hear charges of anti-intellectualism leveled against him.[3] The human mind was to him a wonderful instrument, a delight and a responsibility, perfectly designed for what it was intended. It contributed toward man's freedom, providing him with means for independence within human limits. What it could not provide was direct access to the whole mind or will of God. Speaking then from his own heart, Whittier addressed the emotions of his readers. Women were meant to weep on reading "The Farewell of a Virginia Slave Mother to her Daughters Sold into Southern Bondage." Christians were meant to be indignant on hearing that a Negro on the auction block was recommended by his owner as "a Christian slave." Men of New England were meant to be roused by reminders of how their stalwart ancestors would have acted. The agonizing cry of the soul in bondage, hoarse, horrible, and strong, was meant to haunt the dreams of honest men.

Whittier used words as weapons. They were intended to pierce directly to the heart, and any words would do which served that purpose. His early poems of persuasion, written in the 1830's and 1840's when he was most actively a propagandist, were filled with familiar clichés which tradition guaranteed effective. He turned, he admitted, the crank of an opinion mill to grind out verses one so like the other that often only their titles distinguish them. He used many of the same established phrases which Philip Freneau and Thomas Paine had used effectively years before when they urged men to action during the American Revolution. Rhetorical gestures, such as Fourth of July orators used to make or candidates for election in a political campaign still find useful, beckoned even to readers who could not understand them. Whittier called on each "lover of Peace" to defend "Liberty's dishonored name"; or Justice "balanced in the scale," while "tales of woe," of "brutal lust and fiendish wrong" wring the hearts of all honest men. Even natural objects which Whittier was sometimes to picture with affectionate perception were now stylized, as the "green hills of New England," "Delaware's blue waters," "Massachusetts' rocks of grey," "Hudson's frowning palisades," "Alleghany's laurelled crest."

However successful they may have been in reaching the heart or conscience of Whittier's contemporaries, these verses are now often passed over. They are considered inferior—but not because Whittier's facts were sometimes wrong when he pictured tortured slaves shrieking in agony beneath the whistling whip-lash swung by bestial overseers, nor because he did not mean well or was fanatic or insincere. What cripples them are words and phrases so worn that they provide no friction; they are counters moved about in imitation of perception; they fail to attach themselves to things. The reader is not made to see the rocks or hills or palisades, or even the Negro and his owner who punishes him. He is only told of them, that natural objects exist and are pretty, or that men suffer. A green hill may call up a thousand pleasant associations unconnected with the effect Whittier intended. A frowning palisade may even be momentarily arresting as an image, until it is examined within the context in which it is placed. These pictorial devices, however, were not meant to be examined. They were meant to call forth conventional responses.

III   *The Sting of Words*

William Faulkner speaks of words and phrases of this type as "profoundly without life" because they "go straight up in a thin line"; they are just sounds that people make when they feel strongly at second hand about something which, not having experienced, they cannot really describe. Only a few of Whittier's antislavery poems, such as perhaps "The Farewell of the Virginia Slave Mother," "Massachusetts to Virginia," and "The Christian Slave," can be even tentatively admired. In them force of sincerity and depth of conviction may overweigh the threadbare phrases and the patched, protruding elbows of rhyme and rhythm. What Whittier had to say about slavery was usually said better in his prose in which some substance of argument supported his emotional appeal.

In almost all of the antislavery poems, Whittier's feeling was stronger than his control of language or his ability effectively to dramatize situations. Occasionally, however, his imagination was tenderly touched, as when in 1847 he read in a journal of African exploration of female slaves who sang dolefully through the night, asking of Rubee, their God, "Where are we going?" Their country of Bornou "was a pleasant country, full of all good things; but this is a bad country," they sang, "and we are miserable." Translating to pliant four-stress lines, Whittier rewrote their plaint in "Song of Slaves in the Desert," binding each stanza expertly with linkages of sound and the strong beat of a refrain:

> Where are we going? Where are we going?
> Where are we going, Rubee?
> Lord of people, lord of lands,
> Look across these shining sands,
> Through the furnace of the noon,

Through the white light of the moon,
Strong the Ghiblee wind is blowing,
Strange and large the world is growing!
Speak and tell us where we are going,
    Where are we going, Rubee?

Whittier recognized that most of his antislavery verses were inferior as poetry, but he never really apologized for them. They constituted his pacific contribution to what he often referred to as a moral warfare, a battle against falsehood. They were calls to action, prods to duty, incentives to sympathy, ringing challenges to the unbought farmer, the free laborer, the benevolent churchman. Today, it is probably impossible to gauge their effectiveness. They were often reprinted, but by editors as eager as Whittier to shock readers to emotional response, then to action.

Whittier did better in those later years when, in his forties, he withdrew from the hurly-burly of partisan scrambling in Philadelphia and New York. Almost any poet does better when removed from tumultuous situations in which other people's words distort his own—tempt him to speak as other people speak because he thinks that what he then says will be more easily comprehended. Other voices—those of poets, orators, and propagandists—so often beat on Whittier that he was tardy in recognizing, not *what* he wanted most to say, but *how* to say it. He was never successful at what Henry James was later to call perception at the pitch of passion. Excitement troubled Whittier physically—his nerves went to pieces under it, his heart beat too fast, his head and eyes ached.

Fortunately he was at home in Amesbury when in 1850 he read of Daniel Webster's statesmanlike plea that the North make concessions to Southern demands in order to preserve the union. In the poem which he wrote then and called "Ichabod," he attained heights of effective denunciation not reached before or attempted again. "This poem," Whittier later explained in a headnote in his collected *Writings*, "was the outcome of the surprise and grief and forecast of evil consequences which I felt on reading the Seventh of March Speech of Daniel Webster in support of the 'Compromise' and the Fugitive Slave Law. No partisan or personal enmity dictated it. On the contrary, my admiration of the splendid personality of the great senator was never stronger than when I laid down his speech, and, in one of the saddest moments of my life, penned my protest." He expected readers to be reminded by the title he had chosen of the verse in I Samuel 4:21: "And she named the child Ichabod, saying, the glory is departed from Israel."

"Ichabod" is often compared to Robert Browning's "The Lost Leader," which scolds Wordsworth for having accepted the post of poet-laureate, for leaving his serious fellow poets "just for a handful of silver, . . . Just for a ribbon to stick in his coat." A glance at the two poems together reveals much of both poets. First, it is recalled that Whittier's is usually considered to be one of his better poems, while Browning's is sometimes dismissed as a somewhat ill-tempered, partially quizzical *jeu d'esprit*. Though Browning certainly meant what he said and felt strongly about it, Whittier is more intensely serious and unmistakably sincere. He is more formal and austere, more regular in meter. No reader doubts from the first line onward that Whittier is choked with sorrow. Beside him, Browning may seem frivolous: he speaks with colloquial looseness of a ribbon stuck in a coat, of silver doled out. His anger is not controlled by compassion. "Blot out his name," he shouts. "Let him never come back to us." Browning stands aside from his lines, allowing them to speak humorously, viciously, or in angry dismissal. Whittier in his is a man of sorrow from beginning to end. But each in his manner speaks so movingly that the decision about which is the better poem becomes extremely difficult.

It may be that poems cannot be compared. But Browning seems more surely an artist, in better control of himself and his line, more nimbly free to rhyme or not as the spirit of denunciation moved him. His verses move dramatically toward increasing intensity. They are capped with the release of fresh resolution. The reader is not simply swayed emotionally; he is involved in what Browning has written. He wonders exactly how much of jealousy, how much of anger, how much of mockery—and at whom—the poem really intends. No such ambiguities disturb Whittier's apparently simpler ending which suggests that we look backward to what the man has been rather than at the shame which covers him now. Self-contained, consistent in mood, exact in rhythm, sincere in the noblest sense, Whittier's verses may, however, be thought less interesting than Browning's. It is difficult to read the New England poet's lines aloud without allowing voice or gesture to accomplish what the words themselves should do.

This probably was not true for Whittier's contemporaries who enjoyed declamatory rhetoric and knew their Bibles better than do their descendants. Notley Sinclair Maddox has pointed to subtle intimations of meaning in the last quatrain:

> Then pay the reverence of old days
> To his dead fame;
> Walk backward, with averted gaze,
> And hide the shame.

Most people in Whittier's time would have recognized in these lines an allusion to Genesis 9:20-25, which recounts how Noah planted a vineyard and then "drank of the wine and was drunken; and he was uncovered in his tent," and how his sons Shem and Japheth, apprised of their father's nakedness by their younger brother Ham, went into the tent to cover him ("and their faces were backward, and they saw not their father's nakedness"), but how Ham, having seen the nakedness of his father, was therefore cursed: "a servant of servants shall he be unto his brethren."

Contemporaries would then recall that Daniel Webster, like Noah, had once been a great man who had in such things as his reply to Hayne twenty years before led his people, as if in an ark, to safety. He had, in a figurative sense, planted a great vineyard, but had fallen prey to its fruit. They would have recalled that Webster was notorious as a drinking man, that a potent punch had even been named in his honor. "In thus evoking, with a poignant blending of wry humor and pitying reprehension, the parallel spectacle of great men besotted and fallen," says Mr. Maddox, "Whittier doubtless intended no serious suggestion that Webster's defection was due to overindulgence in alcohol." Rather, as preceding stanzas indicate, "he thought of Webster as a victim of inebriants far more dire—of pride and ambition, under whose fatal corruption he made evil his good."[4]

Further meanings cluster about the stanza because this particular Genesis story was a favorite among people who sought religious sanction for slavery, discovering justification in Ham's unnatural crime and the paternal curse placed on him for the bondage in which his descendants, the Negroes, were held. To use it thus as Whittier used it was daring, and effective. It reminded readers of the brotherhood of him who saw the nakedness of the great man and those who in sorrowful respect for what he had been walked "backward, with averted gaze." Because questions are thus raised about the sharing of guilt and because these questions are not answered, the poem vibrates with implications.

Whittier's use of imagery also identifies "Ichabod" as of a class different from earlier, equally explosive poems. Fallen and lost, the man is withdrawn from the light which had formerly surrounded him, even from the halo-like glory which is remembered as having circled his greying hair. But what the light is which has deserted him, the reader does not immediately know, though he recognizes that its present absence calls forth pitying tears. He who had been a beacon for his time has suddenly extinguished himself; the spotlight of admiration and the inner light of truth are both gone. Angels deride this once-bright soul now deprived of hope and heaven. He has fallen because he dared suggest a judgment contrary to that of God, and that judgment effected the continuing servitude of the descendants of Ham. Having lost man's most precious possession, faith and obedience to God's will, "Then honor dies. The man is dead." The light gone, only spiritual blackness which is power remains.

Whittier's tone throughout is elegiac, but "Ichabod" is not in the conventional sense an elegy. It is rather a dirge, ending without comfort or hope, but with a heartbroken, humane, and commiserating plea for remembrance of this darkened man, not for what he is, but for what he has been. Perhaps no single poem by Whittier sets forth more clearly his hopes for man, his disappointment that most men are not faithful, and his loving kindness which pleads for forgiveness of error.

Drawn thus from Whittier's most profound convictions, well placed within the confines of affective rhyme, bound together by familiar imagery of light and darkness, "Ichabod," in spite of too large a reliance on commonly evocative words like hope and faith and honor, is a poem which anthologists are correct in including in any section reserved for Whittier.

This statement cannot so confidently be made about Whittier's best-known verses of these troublous, divisive times. "Barbara Frietchie" is probably remembered by more people than know who wrote it; it has probably been derided by more critics than have read it; and it has been set to music. Yet, however pummeled about in recitation or recrimination, "Barbara Frietchie" survives; and its most familiar lines were even defiantly parodied in political campaigns almost one hundred years after it was written. Like the "One Hoss Shay," "Rip Van Winkle," and the legend of George Washington and the cherry tree, it lives on at a level where neither literary criticism nor failure of historical verification can harm it. "Shoot if you must," it seems to say, "but spare yourself from any thought that even your most destructive fusillade will do me hurt: tattered and torn, grey-haired or not, I am pretty lively still." Dame Barbara thus becomes embarrassing, particularly because at just the moment she is cast aside as worthless, someone will surely pick her up and cherish her as a curious keepsake. That may be precisely what she is—a curiosity, to be admired, even sheepishly, because, for all her lack of literary respectability, she says something which is pleasant and admirable about brave people anywhere.

Whittier heard the story from Mrs. E. D. E. N. Southworth, a greatly admired popular novelist, who had it at second hand from a neighbor who claimed kinship with the heroine. Whittier turned it immediately to verse for the *Atlantic Monthly,* where it appeared in October, 1863, and from which it was copied widely in other northern periodicals. Some furor was promptly raised. Rival claimants vied for the honor of having said Barbara Frietchie's important words. Other people declared that Whittier in sentimental enthusiasm had invented the entire story. Years later, when someone asked him about it, he attested that he "had a portrait of the good Lady Barbara from the saintly hand of Dorothea Dix, whose life is spent in works of love and duty," and that he had a cane made of wood taken from Barbara Frietchie's cottage sent him by the Maryland historian, Dr. Bernard Steiner. "Whether she did all that my poem ascribed to her or not," Whittier said, "she was a brave and true woman." Scholars since have with reason doubted her authenticity. To most people her existence is irrefutable: Whittier made her.

Some admirers insist that he made her well. Attention is directed to the dramatic structure of the poem, a "perfect rounded dramatic ballad—a miniature," it has been called, "that took thirty practice years—a year for each couplet— to produce spontaneously in white heat at the forge of inspiration." The narrative becomes "a finished drama, consisting of a Prologue, for atmosphere; first, second, third, and fourth acts; epilogue of benediction."[5] Others would divide it to three parts—one, the riotous march, the shuttered streets; two, the pause as the spotlight centers on one attic window where the stars and stripes defiantly wave till shot down, but are even then defended by a brave octogenarian; three, the shamed, shocked silence, the response of the gallant enemy commander, and then the march again, now silent and restrained. It is melodrama, extravagant with gesture, sweetened with ardent love of country and confidence that bravery and patriotism will melt the sternest military heart—and especially when exemplified in a woman, even though she be not fair. Almost every stock element is present, softly molded to conformity with every brave emotion. The ballad strikes exactly the right notes. Read aloud, it can call for response in admiration and resolution. If it receives only laughter, the laughter is embarrassed because it laughs.

Whittier approached more closely to excellence, however, when more restrained. Chief among the objects of attack in the propagandist verse of his most active years had been people who professed to be Christians yet who condoned, even supported, human slavery. Most reprehensible among them were clergymen who quoted from scripture to "sanction crime and robbery and blood." In excess of recrimination Whittier called them "paid hypocrites," "smooth blasphemers," "a mousing priesthood" which from tasseled pulpits bartered truth away, perverting and darkening the searching truth of God. In "Official Piety," he charges that

> Sin in high places has become devout,
>   Tithes mint, goes painful-faced, and prays its lie
> Straight up to Heaven, and calls it piety!
>
> . . . .
>
> Satan is modest. At Heaven's door he lays
> His evil offspring, and, in Scriptural phrase
> And saintly posture, gives to God the praise
> And honor of the monstrous progeny.

In "A Sabbath Scene" he told of a Christian clergyman who came down from his pulpit to help subdue a runaway female slave who had sought refuge in his church. The man of God explains:

> "Although," he said, "on Sabbath Day,
>   All secular occupations
> Are deadly sins, we must fulfill
>   Our moral obligations."

When the slave girl shrieked with terror, her cries were smothered by the altar cloth. She looked in vain about the congregation, "from face to face, For human pity seeking!"

> I saw her dragged along the aisle,
>   Her shackles harshly clanking;
> I heard the parson, over all,
>   The Lord devoutly thanking!
>
> My brain took fire: "Is this," I cried,
>   "The end of prayer and preaching?
> Then down with pulpit, down with priest,
>   And give us Nature's teaching!
>
> "Foul shame and scorn be on ye all
>   Who turn the good to evil,
> And steal the Bible from the Lord,
>   To give it to the Devil!"

IV *And Humor*

When retired from the demands of active partisanship,
Whittier continued the theme more effectively because he
was less shrill in denunciation. In the "Letter from a Missionary of the Methodist Episcopal Church South, in Kansas,
to a Distinguished Politician," written in 1854, his scorn is
not diminished, but something also of humor and ridicule
shows through, and something of language not learned from
books. More than thirty years later Huckleberry Finn would
speak of similar frontier conditions, where brotherly love and
violence became confused. And Whittier spoke now as someone like Huck might have spoken, allowing the emissary of
the church to tell in his own words what happened. No tag
of comment was necessary. The frontier camp meeting opened,

> With prayer, as was most fitting. Half an hour,
> Or thereaway, I groaned, and strove, and wrestled,
> As Jacob did at Penuel, till the power
> Fell on the people, and they cried "Amen!"
> "Glory to God!" and stamped and clapped their hands;
> And the rough river boatmen wiped their eyes;
> "Go it, old hoss!" they cried, and cursed the niggers.
>
> . . . .
>
>   After prayer, the meeting
> Chose a committee—good and pious men—
> A Presbyterian elder, Baptist deacon,
> A local preacher, three or four class-leaders,
> Anxious inquirers, and renewed backsliders,
> A score in all—to watch the river ferry
> (As they of old did watch the fords of Jordan),
> And cut off all whose Yankee tongues refuse
> The Shibboleth of the Nebraska bill.

All things went well in Kansas: "I have lost one negro,"
reported the missionary.

> A first-rate hand, but obstinate and sullen,
> He ran away some time last spring, and hid
> In the river timber. There my Indian converts
> Found him, and treed and shot him.

Beyond that, everything promised to get on splendidly, in large part because of the mission's pious ministrations and works of love. New settlers were arriving,

> and some of them already
> Have purchased negroes, and are settling down
> As sober Christians! Bless the Lord for this!

But even in Eden there was a serpent. The churchman ended his letter with a desperate

> P.S. All's lost. Even while I write these lines,
> The Yankee Abolitionists are coming
> Upon us like a flood—grim, stalwart men,
> Each face set like a flint of Plymouth Rock
> Against our institutions—staking out
> Their farm lots on the wooded Wakarusa,
> Or squatting by the mellow-bottomed Kansas;
> The pioneers of mightier multitudes,
> The small rain-patter, ere the thunder shower
> Drowns the dry prairies.

The good missionary wishes now that he was away from his back-country parish:

> O, for a quiet berth at Washington,
> Snug naval chaplaincy, or clerkship, where
> These rumors of free labor and free soil
> Might never greet me more. Better to be
> Door-keeper in the White House, than to dwell
> Amidst these Yankee tents, that whitening, show
> On the green prairie like a fleet becalmed.

In "The Panorama," Whittier's longest, most comprehensive, and rhetorically most effective political poem, which was read in the fall of 1855 by the Reverend Thomas Starr King at an antislavery meeting at Tremont Temple in Boston, he struck again with satire, now tinged with indignation as he described a slave state frontier village

> straggling in loose disarray
> Of vulgar newness, premature decay;

A tavern, crazy with its whisky brawls,
With *"Slaves at Auction!"* garnishing its walls;
Without, surrounded by a motley crowd,
The shrewd-eyed salesman, garrulous and loud,
A squire or colonel in his pride of place,
Known at free fights, the caucus, and the race;
Prompt to proclaim his honor without blot,
And silence doubters with a ten-pace shot;
Mingling the negro-driving bully's rant
With pious phrase and democratic chant;
Yet never scrupling, with a filthy jest,
To sell the infant from its mother's breast.

He turned his eye scornfully at northern men "of nasal speech
and puritanic hair," who "fatten at the public mill," bartering
decency for profit, "self-sold knaves of gain and peace."
Even when he drew their characters with imperfect lines,
Whittier saw shortcomings among his countrymen as clearly
as anyone of his time.

The sting of satire, as Mark Twain was not many years
later to demonstrate, is not the less because accompanied
with a smile. Whittier was not, as some sedate admirers have
described him, a humorless man. When the Civil War was
over and he watched the hills of his Massachusetts countryside turned by autumn to gold and scarlet in a kind of "sacra-
mental mystery" he wondered more composedly about

Church-goers, fearful of the unseen Powers,
But grumbling over pulpit-tax and pew-rent,
Saving, as shrewd economists, their souls
And winter pork, with the least possible outlay
Of salt and sanctity.

And showing in their daily life

        as little actual comprehension
Of Christian charity and love and duty
As if the Sermon on the Mount had been
Outdated like a last year's almanac.

Neither querulous nor vindictive, these lines from the Prelude to "Among the Hills" exhibit Whittier close to his best. Their sly, observant humor tempts a smile of appreciative, perhaps even guilty, recognition. They contain no posturing, no inflamed rhetoric, no reaching for a response which is only emotional. Readers may smile; they will not laugh.

"God's ways seem dark," said Whittier, and falsehood seemed to rule throughout the land. Whether he expressed his anger in shrill, hot words or in measured contempt, he seems never to have regretted this holy rage which set its foot "upon the lie That man and ox and soul and clod Are market stock to sell and buy!" Certainly truth would triumph and decency reign once more, for God's ways, though dark, were wise and just and merciful. Meanwhile, however, Whittier anticipated Mark Twain's dark condemnation of the whole "damned human race" and T. S. Eliot's later discovery that the waste land of his time was peopled with hollow men when in "For Righteousness' Sake," he charged:

> The age is dull and mean. Men creep,
>   Not walk; with blood too pale and tame
>   To pay the debt they owe to shame;
> Buy cheap, sell dear; eat, drink, and sleep
>   Down-pillowed, deaf to moaning want;
> Pay tithes for soul-insurance; keep
>   Six days to Mammon, one to Cant.

Instead of remaining a fair land of promise, America was hardening into a mold of greed and "strife for place and power," its people lacking "honor, reverence, truth," and presenting, Whittier said in "The Panorama," a scene which required the words of a Milton or a Dante to picture truly. He apologized that his own "harsh numbers" must "grate on tender ears": "No private grief or malice holds my pen."

> Oh, not of choice, for themes of public wrong
> I leave the green and pleasant paths of song,
> The mild, sweet words which soften and adorn,
> For sharp rebuke and bitter laugh of scorn.
> More dear to me some song of private worth,

Some homely idyl of my native North,
Some summer pastoral of her inland vales,
Or, grim and weird, her winter fireside tales
Haunted by ghosts. . . .

Yet he never really gave up hope for his people or his cause. "I will not dream in vain despair," he vowed in "The Waiting":

I wait and watch: before my eyes
    Methinks the night grows thin and gray;
I wait and watch the eastern skies
To see the golden spears arise
    Beneath the oriflamme of day!

Constrained by conscience and ill health from further active part in the struggle for freedom,

Like one whose limbs are bound in trance
    I hear the day-sounds swell and grow,
And see across the twilight glance,
Troop after troop in swift advance,
    The shining ones with plumes of snow!

I know the errand of their feet,
    I know what mighty work is theirs;
I can but lift up hands unmeet
The threshing-floors of God to beat,
    And speed them with unworthy prayers.
.   .   .   .

Oh power to do! Oh baffled will!
    Oh prayer and action! ye are one.
Who may not strive, may yet fulfil
The harder task of standing still,
    And good but wished with God is done!

CHAPTER 7

The Vanished Past

I love the vanished past—love to listen when
The legend of its stirring times is told by aged men—
The hunter's tale of forest deeds—the struggle with the storm—
His battle with the savage bear, a cougar's fearful form.

I love the spell that lendeth to each familiar stream,
The dimness and incoherence of some mysterious dream.
That linketh supernatural things to native hill and glen,
And blendeth with the present view a glimpse of what has been.

—"The Days Gone By"

WHITTIER responded to legendary lore because he liked
good stories similar to those which were told when he
and his family and their visitors gathered about the great
kitchen fire in his boyhood home. He thrilled to tales of
adventure in trapper's hut and Indian camp, of the merry
whirl of dancing among red-capped French Canadians to
the north, of fishing off Boar's Head or among the rocky
waters about the Isle of Shoals, of old-time chowder-parties
and clambakes. He was held spellbound by blood-curdling
accounts of Indian raids and listened enrapt to stories of the
red man's stoic bravery. He responded with enthusiasm to the
rich and picturesque unrhymed poetry, he said, of simple
life and country living—its huskings and sleigh-rides and
apple-bees, its woodcraft mysteries and prodigies of rod and
gun. So much of the romance of New England seemed to
him to be past. The countryside was disturbed no longer, he
lamented in "An Extract from 'A New England Legend,'" by
the Indian's wizard yell nor by witches, ghosts, or goblins:

> The cautious goodman nails no more
> A horseshoe on his outer door,

Lest some unseemly hag should fit
To his own mouth the bridle bit;
The goodwife's churn no more refuses
Its wonted culinary uses
Until, with heated needle burned,
The witch has to her place returned!

He heard with pride of the courage of his ancestors, both Puritan and Quaker, and of the wrath and violence suffered patiently by those among them who strove for freedom to worship or believe as their conscience urged. He learned to recognize harshness and bigotry among the first settlers of New England who sought enforcement of righteousness with sword and scourge, but he found others among them blessed with charity. They were often simple people, like the sea captains who befriended the persecuted Quaker maiden, Cassandra Southwick; or the Boston man who bought, then freed, the Irish girl, Kathleen. For history had usefulness other than the charm of story. Reaching through the past, Whittier found instances fit to inform countrymen of his day of continuing error, but also of inherited humble virtues.

I *Uses of Times Past*

Musing beside the Merrimack, he could forget, he said, the hum and bustle of workaday life, its waste of sin and woe, while simple things—a stone, a mound of earth, a giant tree left standing, a roofless house, decayed, deserted—reminded him of other times when other men lived among these hills and valleys. Remembering was a kind of resurrection. Man owed tremendous debts of gratitude to that within him which allowed him thus to raise the dead past to life. His gift of re-creation through memory or imagination brought man as close as he could approach to God's redemptive power. Retrieving what had been in order to wrest from it what was good was, therefore, a responsibility. These things had once existed and should not die; for, properly remembered, they witnessed to the extent and wisdom of a divine plan. Their restoration, translated to words which other men could understand, could be a service not only to man but to God.

Whittier's notion of the poet's task seldom allowed him to tell a tale for story alone. Even the early "Moll Pitcher" and "Mogg Megone" contain instructive commentary about the inevitable consequences of evil. Seldom, even as a young man, did he submit to the notion that art needed no sanction other than "beauty for its own fair sake"; it owed allegiance also to goodness and eternal truth. The result, in his narrative verse, is a simplified goodness and a simplified truth, measured, he said, "by the breadth of Christian liberty." His bad people seem irredeemably bad and his good unquestionably good. He seldom probed, as Melville or Hawthorne did, toward sources or explanations for evil. It is simply present, susceptible of being flushed away by goodness, which is also there and is patiently awaiting its inevitable recognition.

Not only the New England past was brought to life in Whittier's narrative verse; many subjects came from his reading in European history or in accounts of saints and martyrs everywhere. "The Legend of St. Mark," for example, was inspired by a picture in a book of sacred and legendary art: Tintoretto's sketch for his painting of a tortured Christian slave saved by the intervention of the saint at whose altar he had worshiped. "Barclay of Ury" is a tale of a Quaker's fortitude in Scotland. "Rabbi Ismael" recounts the story of an Israelite priest who, within the Holy of Holies, looked upon the face of his Lord and found it, not stern, but tenderly merciful. "King Volmer and Elsie" was adapted from a Danish writer, Christian Winter; "The Dead Feast of the Kol-Folk" derived from reading in the *Journal of Asiatic Culture;* "The Chapel of the Hermits" from Bernardin Henri Saint-Pierre's *Etudes de la Nature;* and "The Khan's Devil," from a Middle Eastern story.

"Miriam," with Islamic setting, tells a tale "not found in printed books,—in sooth A fancy, with slight hint of truth," written to demonstrate that differing faiths, Moslem and Christian, "agree In one sweet law of charity." "King Solomon and the Ants" is from a legend of the ruler so wise that he "knew The languages of all The creatures great or small That trod the earth or flew"; when his horse was about to step on an ant-hill, Solomon heard the insects speak resignedly of their fate; and, he turned aside in spite of suggestions from his companion, the Queen of Sheba ("comely but black withal"), that such vile creatures should be honored to be stamped to death by so great a man. Recognizing finally the secret of the wise king's worthiness, the dusky Ethiopian queen remarks: "Happy must be the State Whose ruler heedeth more The murmurs of the poor Than flatteries of the great." Few of the early narratives are as clumsily rhetorical as this quotation, but in each a story simple told is capped with a similar enunciation of some noble or pious attitude.

Perhaps best among the poems derived from Whittier's reading is "The Cypress-Tree of Ceylon," which recounts a legend told by Batuba, a Moslem traveler of the fourteenth century, about a sacred tree whose leaves fell seldom; but, when fallen and found and eaten, they had power like the water of Ponce de Leon's fountain to restore youth and vigor. Whittier pictures pious men sitting beneath the tree through weary nights and lingering days, their eyes dimmed to the beauties of nature and the bustle of the world around them as they wait the falling of the restorative leaf. Shall we, he asked, who sit beneath a better tree, whose healing leaves are shed in answer to Christian prayer, be less patient than they? Must the stir of outward things distract us from our vigil? How sternly does the godly man rebuke his erring brother! How easy to wield the sword, as Peter did, to enforce righteousness!

> But oh! we shrink from Jordan's side,
>   From waters which alone can save;
> And murmur for Abana's banks
>   And Pharpar's brighter wave.

Yet eyes need not be dimmed nor the world's work left undone. The poem ends with a prayer addressed to the Saviour who rose from redeeming death to wake his slumbering disciples:

> Bend o'er us now, as over them,
>   And set our sleep-bound spirits free,
> Nor leave us slumbering in the watch
>   Our souls should keep with Thee!

Whittier's popularly effective sermonic manner is here illustrated. An old tale, this time of pagan belief, is used to underscore—to typify, Whittier might have said—the better efficacy of Christian faith. Yet beneath its simplicity of rhyme and line are complexities over which the reader will linger. To understand the first quatrain quoted above, he must recall how Naaman, captain of the host of the King of Syria, a mighty man in valor but a leper, was prepared to do "some great thing" to rid himself of his disease; but how he balked when Elisha instructed him simply to bathe in the waters of Jordan: "Are not Abana and Pharpar, rivers of Damascus, better than all the waters of Israel?" he asked. "May I not wash in them and be clean?"

Meanings then begin to flutter through the poem, which is never completely precise, any more than the symbolism of the tale of Naaman in II Kings 5 is precise. Jordan's water seems to represent simple faith and the rivers which irrigate Damascus' fertile plain worldliness; but the implications of the lines suggest more—not only the proud man humbled, but also the fate of Gehazi who tried to profit from Elisha's healing gift, and how he was punished. So throughout the poem there are intimations of meaning which probe beyond what is said directly. Is it better to remain so blind to everything but faith that the sweet song of birds, the bloom of flowers, and the lithesome dance of maidens go unnoticed? Should concern with personal salvation distract one from noticing the passing gleam of battle flag, or from girding himself to rebuke his erring brethren? What is the relation between pious waiting and instructive action? Whittier suggests answers; first this, then that, but he presents no solution which can be simply paraphrased. It may be suspected that he did not know these answers; and, in this instance, the friction of one question against the other has produced a poem. Like Thoreau, he pleads for wakefulness, for use of man's perceptive power: Let us not slumber. But on the responsibilities of the waking man he is, though less compelling, equally as elusive as the man who lived beside Walden Pond. He has left something for the reader to do.

This imprecision of Whittier, perhaps because linked to the

familiarly affective imprecisions of Christian scripture, is less effective than that of Thoreau, or even of Melville who used biblical lore more sacrilegiously. "The Cypress Tree of Ceylon" is a poem which invites to dedication. Its intention is to inspire. Its counters are ideas, arranged one against the other. More important than the tree, which is never described, or the men who wait beneath it, grim, grey with age and an unidentified sickness, are the abstractions which each signifies. The slumber to be avoided suggests failure to respond to conventional symbols–a bird's sweet song, the thunder of a tropic storm, or the unnamed wrongs pursued by anonymous men. Words are not attached to things, but to generalities. The poem fails finally to please, not because it lacks the complexity of ambiguity, but because it is thus unnecessarily obscure.

Sometimes Whittier's narrative has no identifiable setting, in place or time. "The New Wife and the Old" is the kind of tale which Poe told better: a dead woman intrudes to the marriage bed of her husband and his young second wife to prove that the dead do not forget nor are forgotten, as

> From their solemn homes of thought,
> Where the cypress shadows blend
> Darkly over foe and friend,
> Or in love or sad rebuke,
> Back upon the living look.

But the story is badly managed. The triumph over the proud strength of the man and his jewel-bedecked bride by the work-torn, meekly suffering former wife may be psychologically sound. The memory of her so fills the bridegroom with the cowardice of sin that he shrinks from the whiteness of his young wife's arms. But something goes amiss, even in regard to symbolic effectiveness, when the spotless first wife steals the jewels which her husband has given as a wedding gift to her fair successor. So mild and long-suffering, yet so rapacious? Whittier's point that even in death the meek do inherit good things of the earth might have been better made.

Another arresting poem is "Kathleen," written skillfully in
the measure and spirit of old English balladry:

> There was a Lord of Galaway,
>   A mighty lord was he;
> And he did wed a second wife,
>   A maid of low degree.
>
> But he was old, and she was young,
>   And so, in evil spite,
> She baked the black bread for his kin,
>   And fed her own with white.

The lord had a fair daughter whom her stepmother, in the
manner of traditional story, treated cruelly:

> She clipped her glossy hair away,
>   That none her rank might know,
> She took away her gown of silk,
>   And gave her one of tow,
>
> And sent her down to Limerick town
>   And to a seaman sold
> This daughter of an Irish lord
>   For ten good pounds of gold.

Discovering this betrayal, the lord offered all his riches
and his lands to whoever would bring Kathleen back to
him. A handsome young page responded that he would find
her, but that he desired no reward other than her hand in
marriage. He traveled far and long in search, until finally
he discovered the fair maid in Boston, a bond servant to a
worthy man who refused to accept money for her ransom,
but gave her freely to the young man. They return to Ireland
to live happily ever afterwards by Galway's shore. Though
a Protestant and, in the eyes of Kathleen and her lover, a
heretic, the good American proved that mercy and loving
kindness know neither sect nor creed.

For it was native demeanor and native places and people
that Whittier was most fond of remembering or inventing
tales about. He read widely in the chronicles of New Eng-

land: for history, Edward Winslow's *Relation,* Edward Johnson's *Wonder-Working Providence of Sion's Saviour,* William
Bradford's *History of Plymouth Plantation,* Thomas Morton's
brash *New English Canaan,* and John Jocelyn's *New England's Rarities;* for stories of witchcraft or persecution, Cotton
Mather's *Wonders of the Invisible World* or his giant *Mag-
nalia Christi Americana;* and for Indian lore, Roger Williams'
A Key into the Languages of America. A complete listing of
Whittier's reading would provide a useful bibliography of
colonial history. His best known prose narrative, *Margaret
Smith's Diary,* is so filled with facts drawn from ancient
records that most readers have difficulty knowing where
history leaves off and fiction begins. One of the puzzles
confronting students of colonial poetry, for example, is the
authenticity of the remarkable poem about Lake Champlain,
beginning "This lonesome lake, like to a sea, among the
mountains lies"; Whittier attributes it to Edward Johnson,
but the source has not been found among colonial archives.

Indian lore and Indian tales attracted Whittier as a young
man, either as he read of them in books or as he heard reci-
tations like those recalled in "Haverhill" of

> The terror of the midnight raid,
> The death-concealing ambuscade,
> The winter march, through deserts wild,
> Of captive mother, wife, and child.

But Whittier's poems about Indians are not among his most
successful. Because he seems to have known them only in
story, they remain the Indians of colonial tradition, interpreted
through the rosy haze of nineteenth-century sentimentality.
Like Mogg Megone, who historically was a sachem among
the savage Sacos at the time of King Philip's wars, they were
brave but cruel; quick with knife and gun, quicker with
tomahawk; and proud of the number of scalps "from the
Yenkees torn" which hung from their belts. Fenimore Cooper's
red men were not more alert than Whittier's to the "faintest
shiver of leaf and limb" which betrayed an enemy's presence.
But like Cooper's aged Chingachgook, Whittier's Indians

were prey also to the white man's firewater; and they sometimes lay unmanly and helpless in drunken slumber. They
are either good Indians, stern but just, and friendly to the
white men, as Squanto was; or they are cruel, treacherous, and
proud. Hardly any woman in Whittier's chivalrous opinion
was ever evil, and his Indian maidens were not exceptions.

"The Bridal of Pennacook" tells a tearful tale of female
fidelity, as Weetamoo, lovely daughter of the great chief
Passaconaway, whose hunting grounds stretch from the White
Mountains eastward to the sea, is given in marriage to proud
Winnepurkit, leader of a northern tribe. She is a child of
the forest, strong and free, graceful and lithe, "slight robed,
with loosely flowing hair," a creature of love and laughter:

> Unknown to her the rigid rule,
>   The dull restraint, the chiding frown,
> The weary torture of a school,
>   The taming of wild nature down.
> Her only lore, the legends told
>   Around the hunter's fire at night;
> Stars rose and set, and seasons rolled,
>   Flowers bloomed and snow-flakes fell,
>   unquestioned in her sight.

In contrast, her father is a stern, lone man who melts only
to the innocent warmth and grace of his daughter's joyous
being. A chief among chiefs, at whose command lesser sachems
gather their tribes for the warpath, he rules in regal splendor
from his lodge beside the Merrimack near what is now
Concord in New Hampshire:

> There his spoils of chase and war,
> Jaw of wolf and black bear's paw,
> Panther's skin and eagle's claw,
>   Lay beside his axe and bow;
> And, adown the roof-pole hung,
> Loosely on a snake-skin strung,
> In the smoke his scalp-locks swung
>   Grimly to and fro.

Weetamoo, her father's only solace, reminds him of his dead wife, her mother, in memory of whom, because of the stoic tradition in which Indians are bred, he could shed no tear:

> The Indian heart is hard and cold,
>   It closes darkly o'er its care,
> And formed in Nature's sternest mould,
>   Is slow to feel and strong to bear.

In greater contrast is Winnepurkit, the bridegroom who takes Weetamoo to the wind-swept ledges, cavernous hillsides, and icy waters of his northern home among the Saugus. In him "no warmth of heart, no passionate burst of feeling" ever responds to her smile or wifely ministrations. When she expresses a wish to pay a summer visit to her father in the fairer lands about the Merrimac, her husband allows her to go; but he will not receive her back unless her father sends presents of wampum with her. This the proud chief of Pennacook will not do, and Weetamoo remains at her father's lodge in "home-bound grief and pining loneliness" through weary months of autumn and winter. When spring comes, the "still faithful wife" leaves "her father's door, To seek the wigwam of her chief once more." Her loyalty as a woman, however, exceeds her Indian sagacity; and she disappears beneath the waters of the Merrimack when the frail canoe in which she set out alone is dashed to pieces among the rocks and swirling ice-floes of the swollen stream. Her death is mourned in a funeral song which sorrowful Indian women sing:

> The Dark eye has left us
>   The Spring-bird has flown;
> On the pathway of spirits
>   She wanders alone,
> The song of the wood-dove has died on our shore:
> *Mat wonck kunna-monee!* We hear it no more!

Probably because he realized that such sentimentalized devotion was closer to the tradition of European romance than to the truth about Indian ways, Whittier pretended that the story of "The Bridal of Pennacook" was told by a group of travelers resting at an inn at Conway after a climb of Mt. Washington. Finding among the landlord's books an old chronicle of border wars, each in turn set to verse part of the story told there of the marriage of Weetamoo. Which traveler—the city lawyer, the student of theology, the shrewd merchant or his lovely daughter, or the unnamed narrator who can be supposed to be Whittier—told which portions of the tale cannot be distinguished, any more than in the later *The Tent on the Beach* a reader can in every instance determine which of the vacationing narrators is responsible for which poems there presented. Whittier's conception of the proper use of history as parable justified such imaginative reconstruction by men and women who filled bare outlines of fact with soft coloring. Faithfulness was faithfulness, even in primitive times. Amid harshness and pride and greed, love however loyal can be destroyed. Thus re-created, the vanished past had messages for people of a later day.

II *History Retold*

Whittier probably treated history most effectively in prose, and especially well in *Margaret Smith's Diary*, a quietly instructive story, filled with sound sense and authentic anecdote rather than with excitement. Certainly one of Whittier's writings which should not be forgotten, it is discovered anew in every generation by a fortunate few who are charmed by Whittier's rendering of a young English girl's account of a visit to New England, where, she said, "I was kindly cared for and entertained, and where I have seen so many strange things." During her year in the colony Margaret met many of the great men of Massachusetts: John Eliot, who tutored the Indians; Simon Bradstreet and his wife who wrote poetry; the learned Nathaniel Ward with whom her brother studied at Agawam; Samuel Sewall, who worried because the selling of beer and strong drink was on the increase in the colony; and Michael Wigglesworth, who spoke against "the gay apparel of the young women of Boston, and their lack of plainness and modesty in the manner of wearing their hair." Frightened at the sight of her first Indian, Margaret was pleased to see how acquiescent and friendly Indians became after a gift of Jamaica rum. She visited their wigwams and felt pity for their solemn-faced squaws; but she also heard stories of Indian captivity, even from the lips of a young man who was shortly to die because of hardships and cruelty he had suffered at the hands of the red men. Traveling through the countryside, she discovered many fine things about the western world—that maple syrup was quite as good as treacle, how skillful fishermen were in cutting quids of tobacco with their jack-knives, how fond the Irish were of strong drink, and how filled with superstition colonial countrymen were.

When journeying to the frontier outpost of Strawberry Bank, she stayed overnight with a widow and her three daughters. "I made a comfortable supper of baked pumpkin and milk," said Margaret, "and for lodgings I had a straw bed on the floor, in a dark loft, which was piled well nigh full with corn-ears, pumpkins, and beans, besides a great deal of old household trumpery, wool, and flax, and the skins of animals." In her sleep she inadvertently struck her foot against one of the pumpkins, "which set it rolling down the stairs, bumping hard on every step as it went." The noise awoke the landlady and her daughters who "came fleeing into the corn-loft, the girls bouncing upon my bed and hiding under the blanket, and the old woman praying and groaning, and saying that she did believe it was the spirit of her poor husband" which had gone thumping down the stairs. "As soon as I could speak for laughing," said Margaret, "I told the poor creature what it was that so frightened her; at which she was greatly vexed; and, after she went to bed again, I could hear her scolding me for playing tricks upon honest people."

In such anecdotes Whittier managed a simple, colloquial language not greatly different from what Mark Twain was to use. The humor is straight-faced; even the irony is masked. There was in Salem, reported Margaret, a poor woman named Goody Morse, who was condemned as a witch because she was said to have been seen "flying about in the sun, as if she had been cut in twain, or as if the Devil did hide the lower half of her." Even her daughter turned against her, saying that inasmuch as her mother had "sold herself to the Devil, did she owe her no further love nor service, for as she had made her bed, so must she lie." When the poor creature's sentence was set aside by the governor, "many people, both men and women, coming in from the towns about to see the hanging, be sore disappointed, and vehemently condemn the Governor therein."

No more than Huckleberry Finn, who was to travel through American villages almost two hundred years later, did Margaret moralize often about what she saw. Her brother fell in love with a Quaker girl and suffered for it. Margaret herself was not sure she liked Quakers: "although I do judge them to be a worthy and pious people, I like not their manner of worship, and their great gravity and soberness do little accord with my natural temper and high spirits." She was sorry for them because they were persecuted, so great a number, both men and women, whipped and put into the stocks. "And I once," she said, "beheld two of them, one a young and the other an aged woman, on a cold day in winter, tied to the tail of a cart, going through Salem Street, stripped to their waists, as naked as they were born, and their backs all covered with red whip marks." Drunken Boggs or the Grangerfords did not have their stories more directly told.

Whittier does not seem to have known that poetry must be as well written as prose. When he told the same story of Quakers whipped, half-naked, at the cart-tail in "How the Women Went from Dover," he underlined it then as a tale "of an evil time, When souls were fettered and thought was a crime," and he introduced a brave good man who reproved the constable whose "torturing whip . . . the bare flesh stung." The language is different: it has become literary, inverted, unnatural. The incident is recounted as a reminder to modern women, "at ease in these happier days," that they may "forbear to judge" of their sister's ways. Translated to prose, the words perhaps might speak more clearly, but their meaning would be little different. Poetry, some people have said, is that which is lost in translation. In this instance, very little is lost.

Most ambitious of Whittier's later poems is "The Pennsylvania Pilgrim," written in 1872 as a tribute to colonial Quakers of Philadelphia and particularly to Francis Daniel Pastorius who in 1663, at the invitation of William Penn, brought a colony of his countrymen to Pennsylvania and settled them in what is now called Germantown. Whittier thought it "as good as (if not better than) any long poem I have written." He hoped that it could appear in a volume by itself, as *Snow-Bound* had; for he sometimes thought it more successful than that profitable poem. At first he wanted to call it "The Germantown Pilgrim." James T. Fields suggested instead "Pastorius of Pennsylvania," which Whittier did not like. After some correspondence, they settled together on "The Pennsylvania Pilgrim," Whittier finding in that title "a rather pleasant sounding alliteration."

Perhaps that is what must be said of "The Pennsylvania Pilgrim": it is a pleasant-sounding poem. Whittier filled it with the trappings of an epic; and in the invocation—not to the gods, but to posterity or to the descendants of the patient, valiant men who settled the New World—he asked that new generations never forget the trials and fears which these ancestors had encountered as they hewed homesteads from wild forest lands. Then a prelude begins, in epic fashion,

> I sing the Pilgrim of a softer clime
> And milder speech than those brave men who brought
> To the ice and iron of our winter time
> A will as firm, a creed as stern . . .

The measure chosen for the body of the poem, perhaps with Dante's example vaguely in mind, was a three-line rhymed stanza in iambic pentameter—a meter in which Whittier was seldom conspicuously successful. In spite of attempts to run the sense from one stanza to another, each was so bound within itself by triple-rhyme that the narrative often stumbles forward by jerks and starts and lacks the natural transitions which Whittier managed well in prose.

But Whittier's high estimate of "The Pennsylvania Pilgrim" is understandable. It celebrates a man who was both wise and good, a convert to the Quaker faith and among the first in colonial America to speak openly against slavery:

> Whatever legal maze he wandered through,
> He kept the Sermon on the Mount in view,
> And justice always into mercy grew.

The poem absorbs, as George Arms has observed,[1] everything which Whittier wished to pack into it: homely humor, antiquarian detail, rebukes to New England harshness, and the inception of the antislavery movement. But that is not to say that it is packed well. Whittier explains that free men in that waking time dropped their buckets deep to bring up hidden waters; but he himself, strolling leisurely through Pennsylvania kitchens and woodlands, seems awkwardly a stranger who brings to an unfamiliar scene only what he had learned before. Pennsylvania, that is to say, becomes a suburb of New England, distinguished only because its men enjoyed freedoms denied those who settled amid the ice and iron of Puritan lands. If Whittier drank from the buckets which Pennsylvanians dropped deeply down, the water must have tasted little different from that in the well-house at Amesbury.

What does distinguish "The Pennsylvania Pilgrim" and makes it superior to Whittier's other discursive narrative is the metaphor of seed, sowing, flowering, and harvest which is introduced first in the prelude and then repeated again at intervals throughout the poem. Seed planted in seventeenth-century Germantown promised bright blossoms for men who followed. Like the century plant given William Penn by John Evelyn in England, slowly "year by year its patient leaves unfold." In the last stanzas a glance is directed toward the late eighteenth century, when it is asked of the century plant

> if it flowered at last
> In Bartram's garden, did John Woolman cast
> A glance upon it as he meekly passed?

And, seeing it, was Quaker John Woolman possessed of a "secret sympathy" which lent him hope, strength, and patience? The plant perhaps is mythical, a symbol provided by nature to remind man that "no seed of truth is lost" and that, because of the planting by pious Quakers of Pennsylvania, "from sea to sea such flowers of freedom bloom."

Patient readers will find the narrative sustained, bound together by the strands of imagery of seed and harvest which Whittier wove through it. They will delight in a sprinkling of sedate humor and a muted, calm assurance that these simple things of which the poet speaks are good. But the argument is finally greater than the poetry; of it one must inevitably say what Whittier said of Pastorius' equally aspiring verse: it is native and homely, nourishing

> like the hash
> Of corn and beans in Indian succatash;
> Dull, doubtless, but with here and there a flash

> Of wit and fine conceit,—the good man's play
> Of quiet fancies.

Among those in history whom Whittier liked best to remember were people like Goody Morse, accused of witchcraft. For purposes of poetry he remembered them, not as old, but as young and attractive and thus the more to be pitied. "The Witch of Wenham" tells in ballad measure the story of a gentle maiden imprisoned as a witch until her lover comes riding in the night to rescue her. Verse form and story were both of a kind with which Whittier was most familiar. Simply told, pathos alternating with hints of peril, but lightened by colloquialism and humor, "The Witch of Wenham" is as successful in its kind as anything Whittier attempted. "She chains him with her great blue eyes," says the young man's mother. "She binds him with her hair." Like the Lorelei of German legend,

> She weaves her golden hair; she sings
> Her spell-song low and faint;
> The wickedest witch in Salem jail
> Is to that girl a saint.

Captured, shut up in the garret of an old farmhouse to wait trial, then helped to escape by the young man who caught her as she dropped, Tom Sawyer-like, from the sloping shingled roof outside her window, she mounted the saddle behind her rescuer and rode away:

> Her arms around him twined;
> And noiseless, as if velvet-shod,
> They left the house behind.

Through wild wood's paths and bridgeless streams they fled, till they came to the Merrimack, where an ancient ferryman rowed them to safety on the other side. Charmed by the youth and happiness of the runaway couple, he gave them his benediction as they left him:

> "God keep thee from the evil eye,
>   And harm of witch!" he cried.
>
> The maiden laughed, as youth will laugh
>   At all its fears gone by;
> "He doesn't know," she whispered low,
>   "A little witch am I!"

Perhaps Whittier should have stopped here, but he could not. Seven concluding stanzas tell of the young people's reception among Quakers who welcomed them gladly and with whom they lived happily,

> Until from off its breast the land
>   The haunting horror threw,
> And hatred born of ghastly dreams,
>   To shame and pity grew.

Again the words limp to find syntax which will fit the rhyme, to clip on a moral which, if it had not been before happily implicit in the ballad, now becomes a nuisance.

Favorite among anthologists of Whittier's most characteristic verse is "The Prophecy of Samuel Sewall," which recounts New England's cherished story of the Puritan judge's penitential recantation of sentences which he had passed on people who had appeared before his court accused as witches. Much of the poem is preparatory, telling the history of the wise old man, a "poet who never measured rhyme," and a "seer unknown to his dull-eared time," who placed the law of divine justice above the laws of man and who late in life even condemned human slavery:

> Honor and praise to the Puritan
> Who the halting step of his age outran,
> And, seeing the infinite worth of man
> In the priceless gift the Father gave,

In the infinite love that stooped to save,
Dared not brand his brother a slave!

Musing on the example of Samuel Sewall, Whittier then wrote the judge's prophecy in words to which generations of Yankee patriots have responded with pride and declaimed with earnest dedication:

"As long as Plum Island, to guard the coast
As God appointed, shall keep its post;
As long as salmon shall haunt the deep
Of Merrimac river, or sturgeon leap;
As long as pickerel swift and slim,
Or red-backed perch, in Crane Pond swim;
As long as the annual sea-fowl know
Their time to come and their time to go;
As long as cattle shall roam at will
The green grass meadows by Turkey Hill;
As long as sheep shall look from the side
Of Oldtown Hill on marshes wide,
And Parker River, and salt-sea tide;
As long as wandering pigeons shall search
The fields below from his white-oak perch,
When the barley-harvest is ripe and shorn,
And the dry husks fall from the standing corn;
As long as Nature shall not grow old,
Nor drop her work from her doting hold,
And her care for the Indian corn forget,
And the yellow rows in pairs to set;—
So long shall Christians here be born,
Grow up and ripen as God's sweet corn!—
By the beak of bird, by the breath of frost,
Shall never a holy ear be lost,
But, husked by Death in the Planter's sight,
Be sown again in the fields of light!"

Caught up by the spirit of the prophecy, Whittier concludes:

The Island still is purple with plums,
Up the river the salmon comes,

The sturgeon leaps, and the wild-fowl feeds
On hillside berries and marish seeds,—
All the beautiful signs remain,
From spring-time sowing to autumn rain
The good man's vision returns again!
And let us hope, as well we can,
That the Silent Angel who garners man
May find some grain as of old he found
In the human cornfield ripe and sound,
And the Lord of the Harvest deign to own
The precious seed by their father's sown!

III   *Legend into Verse*

Whittier, however, may be at his best when, unhampered by history, he remade legend into verse, as he did in "Mabel Martin, a Harvest Idyll," which was written almost ten years after his sister's death in memory of her who "loved with us the beautiful and old." Again in simple measure, he tells of the daughter of a woman executed as a witch; she lives unhappily alone, rejected or mocked by her neighbors until she finds protection within the arms of a strong man who loves her. It is an idyll, nothing more; but as one it is softly compelling. At its end, when moonlight falls through great elm boughs onto the pair, secure at last in love, each reader is likely to agree with what the night wind then whispered: "It is well."

Equally effective is "The Double-Headed Snake of Newbury" which derives from contemplation of the serpent which the Rev. Christopher Toppan described to Cotton Mather as having "really two heads, one at each end; two mouths, two stings or tongues." To those who would scoff at the tale, Whittier warned:

Thou who makest the tale thy mirth,
Consider that strip of Christian earth
On the desolate shore of a sailless sea,
Full of terror and mystery,
Half redeemed from the evil hold

Of wood so dreary, and dark, and old,
Which drank with its lips of leaves the dew
When Time was young, and the world was new,
And wove its shadows with sun and moon,
Ere the stones of Cheops were squared and hewn.
Think of the sea's dread monotone,
Of the mournful wail from the pine-wood blown,
Of the strange, vast splendors that lit the North,
Of the troubled throes of the quaking earth,
And the dismal tales the Indian told,
Till the settler's heart at his hearth grew cold,
And he shrank from the tawny wizard boasts,
And the hovering shadows seemed full of ghosts,
And above, below, and on every side,
The fear of his creed seemed verified;—
And think, if his lot were now thine own,
To grope with terrors nor named nor known
How laxer muscle and weaker nerve
And a feebler faith thy need might serve;
And to own to thyself the wonder more
That the snake had two heads, and not a score!

This excellent light verse is well phrased, well rhymed, written with good-humored sense. No wonder then that

Cotton Mather came galloping down
All the way to Newberry town,
With his eyes agog and his ears set wide,
And his marvelous inkhorn at his side;
Stirring the while in the shallow pool
Of his brains for the lore he learned in school,
To garnish the story, with here a streak
Of Latin, and there another of Greek:
And the tales he heard and the notes he took,
Behold! are they not in his Wonder-Book?

Seldom has bumptious Cotton Mather been more soundly given his come-uppance, or his portentous volume of supernatural lore, *Wonders of the Invisible World*, been more expertly ticked off. But the stories which he told "like dragon's

teeth are hard to kill," so that still in New England far beyond
Mather's time

> whenever husband and wife
> Publish the shame of their daily strife,
> And, with mad cross-purpose, tug and strain
> At either end of the marriage chain,

Then people say, "Look! . . . One in body and two in will,"
the double-headed snake is living still.

Whittier never did so well with legend as in "Skipper
Ireson's Ride," a story told him as true by a schoolmate at
Haverhill Academy. He is said to have begun putting it to
verse as early as 1828, but almost thirty years passed before
he completed it and sent it off to James Russell Lowell for
the *Atlantic Monthly* in 1857. He described it then as "a bit of
Yankee ballad, the spirit of which pleases me more than the
execution." Yet it is the execution—precise, graphic and dramatic, without a wasted word—which allows some readers
to consider this poem Whittier's masterpiece and the best
American ballad of the nineteenth century. It begins, as
many well-told tales do, with the action under way. Old Floyd
Ireson, because of his hard heart, has been tarred and feath-
ered and is being carried on a cart by the women of Marblehead.

That is all the reader is told, except that the narrator thinks
that Floyd's ride was the strangest since the birth of time.
Now, dripping with feathers, "ruffled in every part," the
unfortunate Floyd looks like the "Body of turkey" with "head
of owl," with his "wings a-droop like a rained-on fowl," while
"scores of women, old and young, Strong of muscle and glib
of tongue" push and pull the cart in which he stands; they
move it steadily up the rocky Salem road, while they shout
and sing the shrill refrain, which this time is not written as it
had been at the end of the first stanza in the smoothly correct
accents of the narrator, but in Marblehead dialect:

> Here's Flud Oirson, fur his horrd horrt,
> Torr'd an' futherr'd an' corr'd in a corrt
> By the women of Morble'ead!

What a pack of women they were: "wrinkled scolds with hands on hips," young girls "in bloom of cheek and lips,"

> Wild-eyed, free-limbed, such as chase
> Bacchus round some antique vase,
> Brief of skirt, with ankles bare,
> Loose of kerchief and loose of hair.

Whittier calls them Maenads, sea-nymphs, singing to the accompaniment of "conch-shells blowing and fish-horns' twang."

Only with the fourth stanza does the reader learn the reason for the riot. The narrator then interrupts the procession to explain that Floyd Ireson was a sea captain, a native of Marblehead, who had sailed his vessel away from a sinking ship manned by his own townspeople and had left them to drown amid the fog and rain of stormy Chaleur Bay. Why he had done it is not revealed. It can be suspected that the crew of the stricken ship had done better than he on some former fishing expedition; for, in the one bit of dialect in these two expository stanzas, Ireson is reported to have shouted,

> "Sink or swim!
> Brag of your catch of fish again!"

Whittier is seldom so succinct or so successful. He approaches pathos, but only for a moment, when he thinks of the mothers, sisters, wives, and daughters of the sailors so cruelly deserted. They watch "over the moaning rainy sea . . . For the coming that might not be." And not only they, but the whole town—"sharp-tongued spinsters, old wives grey," and "sea-worn grandsires"—join the mob around the cart in which Floyd Ireson rode, dishonored. They shook

> head, and fist, and hat, and cane
> And croaked with curses the hoarse refrain.

And the refrain is again in the dialect of Marblehead, harsh and bitterly recriminating.

Then suddenly the mood of the poem changes, as the beauty

of orchard and lilac beside the Salem road contrasts with the grim spectacle of hatred and revenge. Floyd Ireson speaks for the first time: "Hear me neighbors!" He speaks as one of them, a fellow-townsman, a neighbor still, though held in contempt and made to appear less than human by his garment of feathers and tar. Humiliated and degraded, he is still a man. What, he asks,

> What is the shame that hides the skin
> To the nameless horror that lives within?

Awake or asleep, he remembers that dreadful scene at sea. He is haunted by the cries of the sailors he had callously deserted to certain death. His crime was the crime of any man who turned away from his suffering fellows. "Hate me and curse me," he cries,

> "I only dread
> The hand of God and the face of the dead."

Touched by his words, half in pity, half in contempt, the women set him free. They gave him a cloak to cover the shame which they had smeared on him, and then left him alone: "God has touched him!" they said, "Why should we!" The punishment which fitted his crime was not to be provided by human hands.

The wild anger of the women is moderated to compassion mixed with scorn. It is not they but the narrator who transforms their mad, revengeful refrain to contemplative commentary. No longer is it "Old Floyd Ireson," but "Poor Floyd Ireson" who is carried on the cart by the women of Marblehead. The ballad succeeds because of its effective dramatic structure, its handling of details of locale and character, and its balance of colloquial with traditional literary diction. Of all the rides "told in story or sung in rhyme," this, said the narrator, was the strangest. What begins in a spirit of mockery, compared lightly to Apuleius' "Golden Ass" and "one-eyed Calender's horse of brass," suddenly becomes drama, filled with movement, noise and shouting. Just as suddenly it then moves toward a climax in which action ceases, to be replaced by realization that Floyd Ireson's brief ride in Marblehead can in truth be compared with fabled "rides since the birth of time." The refrain which ends each stanza becomes at last, as John Pickard has said so well, a mournful dirge forever accusing and dooming poor Floyd Ireson who lives on when his story is ended—a tragic figure who "towers over the drama, acting without apparent justification, and then vanishing to live alone with his shame and remorse."[2] No tag of moral is needed; because suggestions of meaning are organic to the poem, they inevitably emerge without obtrusive prodding by the narrator.

Historians of Marblehead have complained that the legend is distorted, that it was not Captain Ireson, but someone of quite another name who was punished by his townspeople, and not in just this manner. But Whittier was not writing history, any more than he was in *Margaret Smith's Diary,* or than Melville was in *Israel Potter* or than Hawthorne was in "The Maypole of Merrymount" or *The Scarlet Letter.* Equally unimportant is knowledge that in the *Arabian Nights* it was not "one-eyed Calender" who had a horse of brass; it is also insignificant that Lowell contributed importantly to "Skipper Ireson's Ride" by correcting the refrain, as it appears in all but the first and the last two stanzas, to give it the peculiar accent of Marblehead speech. For whatever aid he received or however his imagination amended facts of history or legend, Whittier perhaps for the first time and at the age of fifty made a poem which was organically whole. He was sometimes to do as well again, but seldom better.

Twenty years later in "The Henchman" he produced a narrative ballad of courtly love which Winfield Townley Scott is correct in placing also among Whittier's best: "His purity of line, its chaste control of the art of lyric singing make it truly beautiful."[3] The first stanza and the last give some impression of the whole; but the poem should be read entire as an illustration of how Whittier, when he forgot his preachments, could write with simple effectiveness of matters which strike close to the heart:

> My lady walks her morning round,
> My lady's page her fleet greyhound,

My lady's hair the fond winds stir,
And all the birds make songs for her.
. . . .

No lance have I, in joust or fight,
To splinter in my lady's sight;
But at her feet, how blest were I
For any need of hers to die!

CHAPTER *8*

Flemish Pictures

But my thoughts are full of the past and old,
I hear the tales of my boyhood told;
And the shadows and shapes of early days
Flit dimly by in the veiling haze,
With measured movement and rhythmic chime,
Weaving like shuttles my web of rhyme.

—"The Prophecy of Samuel Sewall"

A S MUCH AS HE LOVED the New England of history
and legend, Whittier loved best the New England of
his own time, especially of his youth. Like Stephen Vin-
cent Benét, he was charmed by the sound of old American
names, and decorated his verses with them: Moosehillock.
Kearsarge, Sunapee, Winnepisogee, Pemigewasset, Monadnock. He liked native ways of saying words, rhyming "lion"
with "iron," "Martha" with "swarthy" and "worthy," "calling"
with "broiling," "shadows" with "meadows" and "ladders,"
"timbers" with "embers." He found reminders of romance in
the sight of boatmen on the river, the sound of huntsmen
among the woods or meadowlands, in the clang of anvil or
the creak of water-wheel. He liked to recall the chatter of
wild geese, the laugh of the loon, the lonely plaint of the
whippoorwill. He thought of beaver cutting timber with
patient teeth, of minks that were fish-wards, of crows as
surveyors of highways. His verses are densely planted with
birches and scarlet maples, hemlock, oak, and lilac. Wild
grapes border his brooks, lilies blossom in his ponds, brown
nuts and violets are scattered over his hills. He recalled the
sumptuous fare of old-time feasts:

small wild hens in the reed-snares caught
From the banks of Sondagardee brought;

Pike and perch from the Suncock taken,
Nut from the trees of the Black Hills shaken,
Cranberries picked in the Squanscot bog,
And grapes from the vines of Piscataquog.

I *Precursor of Robert Frost*

Few poets have written as successfully as Whittier of nature without man in it. "With the sureness that plain simple vision gives to the imperfect craftsman," John Macy has said, "he made pictures of his landscape that are unsurpassed, if not unsurpassable."[1] His wistfully tender verses of place are as indigenous as the trees and wildflowers and harvests which they describe. His genius, said Francis Parkman, drew its nourishment from native soil.[2] Not until Robert Frost began to write of birches and stone walls and snow-filled New Hampshire woods was another to do as well. When Whittier's poems of countryside are no longer read with pleasure, then, it has been said, the last Yankee will have died.

Sometimes, as in "The Fruit-Gift," written late when his language was maturely under control, Whittier contemplated the lush and clustered sweetness of nature's product,

Full-orbed and glowing with the prisoned beams
Of summery suns, and rounded to completeness
By kisses of the south-wind . . . ,

to find in it reminders of finer and even fuller beauties which man once knew in Eden but which now must be imagined through analogy. Musing over the gift of fruit—grapes, perhaps, or an ear of golden corn—which had been sent to him,

I said, "This fruit beseems no world of sin.
Its parent vine, rooted in Paradise,
O'ercrept the wall, and never paid the price
Of the great mischief,—an ambrosial tree,
Eden's exotic, somehow smuggled in,
To keep the thorns and thistles company."
Perchance our frail, sad mother plucked in haste
A single vine-slip as she passed the gate,

> Where the dread sword alternate paled and burned,
>   And the stern angel, pitying her fate,
> Forgave the lovely trespasser, and turned
> Aside his face of fire; and thus the waste
> And fallen world hath yet its annual taste
> Of primal good, to prove of sin the cost,
> And show by one gleaned ear the mighty harvest lost.

For Whittier's descriptive verse, no more than Robert Frost's, was not written simply for description's sake. His landscape had people in it; and, usually good people, their activities were meant to supply meaning to the scene. In the Prelude to "Among the Hills," composed in 1869 at the peak of his late-maturing powers, Whittier spoke of himself as

>   a farmer's son
> Proud of field-lore and harvest-craft, and feeling
> All their fine possibilities, how rich
> And restful even poverty and toil
> Become when beauty, harmony, and love
> Sit at their humble hearth.

He remembered, however, that among New England's stone-filled farmlands toil was often wearisome, that bodies tired and hearts were starved even among the plenitude of nature. Like Hawthorne and William Faulkner, he invoked images of nature untended which irresistibly overcame the husbandry of man. Looking back over half a century, he recalled

>   old homesteads where no flower
> Told that the spring had come, but evil weeds,
> Nightshade and rough-leaved burdock in the place
> Of the sweet doorway greeting of the rose
> And honeysuckle, where the house walls seemed
> Blistering in sun, without a tree or vine
> To cast the tremulous shadow of its leaves
> Across the curtainless windows, from whose panes
> Fluttered the signal rags of shiftlessness.

Part of the poverty of New England was poverty of the spirit. Many of its strongest people had adventured westward to new lands and less rocky fields. But New England was not desolate; only its people were. Amid rich woodlands and half-tilled fields they lived a pinched, bare, and comfortless existence. Within the farmhouses of New England

>   the cluttered kitchen floor, unwashed
> (Broom-clean I think they called it); the best room
> Stifling with cellar-damp, shut from the air
> In hot midsummer, bookless, pictureless
> Save the inevitable sampler hung
> Over the fireplace, or a mourning piece,
> A green-haired woman, peony-cheeked, beneath
> Impossible willows; the wide-throated hearth
> Bristling with faded pine-boughs half concealing
> The piled-up rubbish at the chimney's back;
> And, in sad keeping with all things about them,
> Shrill querulous women, sour and sullen men,
> Untidy, loveless, old before their time,
> With scarce a human interest save their own
> Monotonous round of small economies
> Or the poor scandal of the neighborhood.

Blind to beauty everywhere about them, these people lived crippled lives as prisoners, cramped and starved, Whittier said, while Nature spread a feast of joy and wonder all about them. This should not be:

> Our yeoman should be equal to his home
> Set in fair, green valleys, purple walled,
> A man to match his mountains, not to creep
> Dwarfed and abased below them.

Like Emerson and Thoreau, each of whom years before had spoken similar words, perhaps more effectively, Whittier would invite his countrymen to look freshly on their world with their eyes and hearts to feel the "beauty and the joy within their reach." He would recall the simple pleasures of "Home and home loves, and the beatitudes Of nature." His ministering gift to them and to all people was to remind them of what they had been and might be, to help them recognize in nature the

outward types and signs
Of the eternal beauty which fulfills
The one great purpose of creation, Love.

Yet no matter how often Whittier cautioned himself that in the "beautiful present the past is no longer needed," he seemed as he grew older increasingly to find in nature mementos of the passing of time. In "The Last Walk in Autumn" he told of wandering through hilly woodlands beneath bare boughs outstretched as if pleading with the leaden skies. Beside the Merrimack he saw that

The withered tufts of asters nod;
And trembles on its arid stalk
The hoar plume of the goldenrod,
And on the ground of sombre fir,
And azure-studded juniper,
The silver birch its buds of purple shows,
And scarlet berries tell where bloomed the sweet
wild-rose.

As he walked, he thus looked about to see, much as Thoreau had, each fair embodiment of nature clearly; but he did not write about his observations so well as the Concord walker. Whittier often allowed adjectives to do too much of his descriptive work for him; but, in these lines and in others like them, he captured something of the grey bleakness of approaching winter in New England, which reminded him of the approaching winter of his life. Living quietly now in Amesbury, with books and friends, he remembered visits from Emerson, "who might Plato's banquet grace," and Longfellow, the "gentle pilgrim troubadour, Whose songs have girded half the earth." He knew not, he said, "how in other lands The changing seasons come and go." New England brought him happiness enough:

Here dwells no perfect man, sublime,
Nor women winged before their time,
But with the faults and follies of the race,
Old home-bred virtues hold their not unhonored place.

Remembering these home-bred virtues, he would sing, not the harsh songs of persuasion which he formerly had sung, but simpler melodies; and he hoped that they might reach the homes and hearths, he said, even of those who had disagreed with his partisan verses. In "Mountain Pictures" he wrote of a "brown old farm-house like a bird's-nest hung" upon the side of Mount Monadnock:

> The bucket plashing in the cool, sweet well,
> The pasture bars that clattered as they fell;
> Dogs barked, fowls fluttered, cattle lowed; the gate
> Of the barnyard creaked beneath the merry weight
> Of sun-brown children, listening while they swung,
> The welcome sound of supper-call to hear;
> And down the shadowy lane, in tinklings clear,
> The pastoral curfew of the cow-bell rung.

If recollection of Samuel Woodworth's "Old Oaken Bucket" and Oliver Goldsmith's "The Deserted Village" both intrude between many readers and complete appreciation of these lines, the lines nonetheless succeed in setting forth, even in the faded colors of an old daguerreotype, a picture which evokes quiet emotion. Against such backgrounds of forest or hillside or farm were to be set the New England pastorals which Whittier had called for many years before and which now, as he approached fifty, he would attempt seriously to produce.

II *Democratic Pastorals*

Sentimentality was to tint almost all of those later genre sketches done from observation or memory of incidents of everyday life. Even when he wrote of them in prose, as in "Schoolday Remembrances" or in reminiscence of "The Fish I Didn't Catch" or of carefree "Yankee Gypsies" who roamed the countryside of his youth, they were colored with an almost doleful assurance that these things which once were and which he knew and loved were now gone and would not return. What distinguishes them all is that they were drawn from scenes and models which Whittier had known. He did not now, like Longfellow or even Lowell, attempt to elevate the taste of his contemporaries by presenting them with home-made copies of style or subject imported from other lands. Winfield Townley Scott is correct in suggesting that in this "lay his chief differences from the countrymen with whom he is mostly closely connected—Longfellow, Lowell, Holmes; and here, too, the mainspring of his superiority over them. Where they were often wooden, he was natural."[3] There is something clear and authentic about Whittier, Ludwig Lewisohn once said, "something of brooks and trees rather than of horse-hair furniture and antimacassars."[4] Whittier produced, said another commentator, "the sort of verse which appealed, first of all, to his neighbors."[5]

In that sense he can be thought of, even more than the self-conscious Whitman, as a democratic poet. He was the kind of poet, descended from simple ballad singers of all time, who made the kinds of verse which his listeners wanted to hear. Though the voice of the people may be loud and in many matters undoubtedly finally right, its ear is often faulty, its senses lulled by what it wishes to feel. "The Barefoot Boy," which is perhaps after "Barbara Frietchie" Whittier's best-remembered poem, represents an example of just this point. Though twenty years older than Tom Sawyer, Whittier's little man with turned-up pantaloons has appealed to much the same kind of sentimental reconstruction of past days as Mark Twain's ragged urchin. Either barefoot boy, fishing pole on shoulder, scuffling carefree through the dust of summer, might have sat model for the other; and which is more sentimentally realized would be difficult to determine. There are differences, of course; and these are explained, in part, by differences in the total experience of Whittier and Samuel Clemens and, in greater part, by the circumstance that in his book Mark Twain built parts more skillfully into an organic whole. But the dissimilarities are probably also as correctly explained by the differences between what appealed to people in 1855, when "The Barefoot Boy" first appeared, and what appealed to another generation which applauded Tom Sawyer with an appreciation not unsimilar to that which even later greeted the hard-bitten sentimentality of Holden Caulfield in *The Catcher in the Rye*. Each work—or each youth—reproduced in terms of its time what readers best wanted to recall of certain superiorities which boyhood offered. In its way, each celebrated the "clouds of glory" which Wordsworth had said surround the child who with sad inevitability is father to the man.

Hedged about by moral restrictions, Whittier in the 1850's narrowed and intensified the focus of his imagination. If once he had thought of poetry as an end in itself and had asked in youthful prayer that his soul be quickened by "fancy's pure imaginings," he was now certain that, when not grounded solidly on the rock of humanitarian ethics, "Art builds on sand." But he had also discovered that, even dedicated to the service of man, poetry could be dangerous and difficult to control: it could lead men toward war, as his militant verses seemed to. As he grew older, Whittier appears to have distrusted imagination, especially those "bolder flights that know no check." It was better, he said in "The Tent on the Beach,"

> to use the bit then throw
> The reins all free on fancy's neck.
> The liberal range of Art should be
> The breadth of Christian liberty,
> Restrained alone by challenge and alarm
> When its charmed footsteps tread the border land of harm.

Invention was dangerous, art was suspect, for the most sincerely made contrivance of man failed to encompass the largeness of the divine, eternal plan. How impious and audacious of man to believe that he could create! Perhaps the best he could do, Whittier thought, was to remember and to reproduce—as Wordsworth had suggested—simple emotions recollected now in mature tranquility. Memory was indeed a kind of imagination, and reconstruction of scenes and events and people recalled from his past a poet's legitimate task. Late in life Whittier confessed, "If not the wisest, it appears to me the happiest people in the world are those who still retain something of the child's creative faculty of imagination, which makes atmosphere and color, sun and shadow, and boundless horizons, out of what seems to prosaic wisdom most inadequate material."[6]

In "The Barefoot Boy" Whittier spelled this out with direct simplicity: the "painless play," the "laughing day" of boyhood, the "Health that mocks the doctor's rules" and "Knowledge never learned in schools"

> Of the wild bee's morning chase,
> Of the wild-flower's time and place,
> Flight of fowl and habitude
> Of the tenants in the wood;
> How the tortoise bears his shell,
> How the woodchuck digs his cell,
> And the ground-mole sinks his well;
> How the robin feeds her young,
> How the oriole's nest is hung;
> Where the whitest lilies blow,
> Where the freshest berries grow,
> Where the ground-nut trails its vine,
> Where the wood-grape's clusters shine;
> Of the black wasp's cunning way,
> Mason of his walls of clay,
> And the architectural plans
> Of gray hornet artisans.

The poem does not probe deeply. Until its final twenty lines, it is simply a remembrancer: "From my heart I give thee joy,—I was once a barefoot boy." Then the mood changes:

> Cheerily, then, my little man,
> Live and laugh, as boyhood can!

All too soon those bare feet must be shod, imprisoned by adult pride, threatened by treacherous sands of sin. How simply it is said, yet nothing in the poem is fresh or new, except the buoyant boyhood memories! The moral thrust at the end becomes bathos. At just about this time Walt Whitman was contemplating a childhood reminiscence of another barefoot boy who walked and talked with nature as cheerily as Whittier's did; but he became the man who produced in "Out of the Cradle Endlessly Rocking" one of America's few great poems. It was at this time also that Whittier is said to have thrown a copy of Whitman's *Leaves of Grass* in disgust into the fire.

Published in the same year as "The Barefoot Boy," Whittier's companion tale—and a better poem—of "the barefoot maiden," "Maud Muller" has not fared so well with readers. The story is well formulated and told with an economy of phrase unusual in Whittier; Wordsworth at his lowliest seldom managed meter better. The first thirty-four lines are straight, objective narrative: they tell of the Judge, an urbane man, riding his chestnut mare through the countryside, where

> Maud Muller on a summer's day
> Raked the meadow sweet with hay.

Stopping for a cup of water from the spring that flows through the meadow, he gallantly compliments and honestly admires the "simple beauty and rustic health" of the country girl; and she, forgetting her bashfulness, talks to him of simple, country things. Then the narrative pauses for thirty lines in which the reader is allowed to hear the thoughts which pass through the minds of each. After the Judge has ridden away, Maud says to herself:

> "Ah me!
> That I the Judge's bride might be!
>
> "He would dress me up in silks so fine,
> "And praise and toast me at his wine.
>
> "My father would wear a broadcloth coat;
> "My brother should sail a painted boat.
>
> "I'd dress my mother so grand and gay,
> "And the baby should have a new toy each day."

And the Judge, as he returns to his duties in the town, also ponders about the simple joys which might ensue if

> "she were mine, and I to-day,
> "Like her a harvester of hay."

Years then pass; and, in a third section, the Judge is pictured as successful in every worldly way—the owner of a fine house, a leader among men, and wedded to

> a wife of the richest dower,
> Who lived for fashion, as he for power,

while Maud remained a country woman, a household drudge married to

> a man unlearned and poor,
> And many children played round her door.

Yet often at the end of a weary day, he, before his marble fireplace, and she, spinning beside her humble hearth, recall their brief meeting; each vaguely wonders whether his life might have been happier if he had succumbed to the romantic impulse which had held him then. Finally, the story told, Whittier takes over to comment with choked voice:

> God pity them both! and pity us all,
> Who vainly the dreams of youth recall.

> For of all sad words of tongue or pen,
> The saddest are these: "It might have been!"

It may be, as George Arms has suggested, that the sadness of these lines "points as much to the thoughtless reader's wish fulfillment as to Maud's recrimination."[7] Their soft sentiment, however, is capped by a pious benediction which even to discriminating readers of Whittier's time must have made the poem seem to end in a whimper. The poet sighs as he finishes the tale—as if in an aside, he suggests that perhaps we all in some future life will discover the happiness which has eluded us on earth:

> Ah, well! for us some sweet hope lies
> Deeply buried from human eyes;

> And, in the hereafter, angels may
> Roll this stone from its grave away.

Why does a poem which presents so simple a story of a not uncommon human predicament seem to fail so utterly? Sentiment is not of itself destructive; for as managed by Wordsworth or Tennyson, or even by Scott Fitzgerald or Sherwood Anderson, it can surround a subject with an evanescent glow of tenderness. But this subtle mood is difficult beyond all others to maintain; it must withstand the brighter light of logic if it is not to tumble into grotesque caricature of itself. The mawkishness of "Maud Muller" is nowhere more effectively exposed than in the parody-sequel which Bret Harte wrote sixteen years later in "Mrs. Judge Jenkins." In this retelling of the story the Judge returns to see his country maid.

> And ere the languid summer died,
> Sweet Maud became the Judge's bride.
>
> But on the day that they were mated,
> Maud's brother Bob was intoxicated;
>
> And Maud's relations, twelve in all,
> Were very drunk at the Judge's hall.
>
> And when the summer came again,
> The young bride bore him babies twain;
>
> And the Judge was blest, but thought it strange
> That bearing children made such a change;
>
> For Maud grew broad and red and stout,
> And the waist that his arm once clasped about
>
> Was more than he now could span; and he,
> Sighed as he pondered ruefully,
>
> How that which in Maud was native grace
> In Mrs. Jenkins was out of place;
>
> And thought of the twins, and wished that they
> Looked less like the men who raked the hay
>
> On Muller's farm, and dreamed with pain
> Of the day he wandered down the lane.

Bret Harte was not so good a man as Whittier, nor had he such good intentions. His verses are languid and his phrasing not so perfected as that of the older man; but, even though leaning on what Whittier had done, he wrote a better poem, ending it with slashing finality:

> If, of all words of tongue or pen
> The saddest are, "It might have been,"

More sad are these we daily see:
"It is, but hadn't ought to be."

Only two years after his pair of barefoot poems, Whittier reached close to the height of his poetic achievement with "Skipper Ireson's Ride" and a few months later, with "Telling the Bees." Both derived from legends he had heard as a younger man and both are included in his collected edition among the "Narrative and Legendary Poems"; but there is a tone of personal involvement in the second poem which makes it seem more proper to consider it, at least in part, as a reconstruction of experience which Whittier had known. "Telling the Bees" is among the few of Whittier's better poems written in the first person; and is almost the only poem written with the simple directness characteristic of his best prose. The opening lines have the same quality of quiet conversation which Robert Frost was later to manage so well in such a poem as "Stopping by Woods on a Snowy Evening." The scene which Whittier describes is in almost every detail that of the farmyard of the house in Haverhill in which he had lived as a boy:

> Here is the place; right over the hill
> > Runs the path I took;
> You can see that gap in the old wall still,
> > And the stepping stones in the shallow brook.

> There is the house, with gate red-barred
> > And poplars tall;
> And the barn's brown length, and the cattle-yard,
> > And white horns tossing above the wall.

The background is thus set forth in simple impressionistic strokes, with adjectives economically and expertly placed. Permanence and solidity pervade the scene, as if it had always been just this way and always would be. The bee hives stand in a row beneath the sun as they had always stood. Only down by the brook is there any change; there the pansies and daffodils, roses and pinks are overrun with weeds; why the reader does not know, except that they are

described as "her poor flowers." Who "she" is is not revealed.
A year has passed, and slowly, since something had happened,

> And the same rose blows, and the same sun glows,
>   And the same brook sings of a year ago.

> There's the same sweet clover-smell in the breeze;
>   And the June sun warm.

The mood hints of sadness, but also of serenity. The linkage
of sound in assonance and controlled alliteration and the
repetition of the word "same," which re-enforces the atmosphere of solid permanence, and the slowing of cadence
achieved in the line about the June sun contribute toward
the creation of sentiment unspoiled by excess.

The narrator then remembers how a year before he had
come courting to that place, carefully brushing the burrs
from his best coat, smoothing his hair, and refreshing himself—the reader supposes after a dusty walk through the
hot summer countryside—at the brook which flowed beside
the farmyard gate. He had not been there for a month, but
little was changed since his last visit. Sunlight slanted through
the leaves; her roses bloomed as they had bloomed a month
before. But the bee hives were different—passing among
them walked a young servant girl, draping each hive with
black and crooning softly to the bees. The narrator knew
enough of Essex custom to realize the significance of this
action. Someone had died, and local superstition required
that the bees be informed immediately to keep them from
swarming from their hives to seek a new home. His heart
went out to Mary, named now for the first time as the young
lady he had come to see. He thought of her unhappiness,
weeping as she must be over the death of a loved one,
perhaps her aged grandfather. But then he heard her dog
whining and, looking more closely toward the farmhouse,
saw that

>   on the doorway sill,
>   With his cane to his chin,
> The old man sat; and the chore-girl still
>   Sung to the bees stealing out and in.

Only with the last stanza does the reader surely know the cause of the young man's quietly modulated grief, held close and almost inarticulate, as a countryman's grief can be:

> And the song she was singing ever since
> In my ear sounds on:—
> "Stay at home pretty bees, fly not hence!
> Mistress Mary is dead and gone!"

No more than in "Skipper Ireson's Ride" or "The Hench-man" is a moral appended, or needed. The solemn elegiac tone, the emotional control, the serene knowledge that beyond the permanence of personal grief is the permanence of memory and custom and place are effectively, even artlessly present, without need for underlining statement. Some readers find that the final stanzas fall below the standard set by the first, that the grief of the narrator is too muted and unrelieved to be convincing. To others, narrative and mood move hand in hand to produce the one flawless poem which Whittier wrote. Most will agreed with John Pickard that "Telling the Bees" succeeds "because of the utter simplicity of its prose-like phrasing and ballad meter, and because of its firm structural unity created by the progression from assurance to fear and then surprise."[8] Whittier himself wondered whether what he thought of as simplicity in the poem might not be interpreted as silliness by others.

Allied in theme to "Telling the Bees" is "My Playmate," which Tennyson is reported to have called "a perfect poem" —and to have added in prophecy that "in some of his descriptions of scenery and wild flowers" Whittier would rank with Wordsworth.[9] But the beauty of the commonplace set forth in colloquial directness to create the mood of quiet sub-mission characteristic of Whittier's best work is smothered in this second poem by the bathos of its theme which simply restates the familiar plaint of lonesome lovers: "Now that we have parted, do you ever think of me?" Even the wild grapes, the brown nuts, the violets, the dark pines, and the summer roses of New England woven through the tapestry of retro-spective narrative succeed only briefly in supplying color to its irresponsible formlessness of design.

For all his crying down of art, Whittier succeeded only when, consciously or not, he provided some kind of structural foundation for his poems, as he had in "Ichabod," in "Telling the Bees," and in "Skipper Ireson's Ride." In many of his attractive poems, he is a poet of phrases or of a few lines or stanzas. He can be made to sound better in quotation of parts then in reproductions of complete poems. The familiar hymn which begins "Immortal love, forever full, Forever flowing free" is a reduction to five of the thirty-three stanzas of "Our Master," the poem from which it is taken. Most of his poems are too long for what they have to say. Even his most devoted admirers must often skip judiciously if they are to make him appear at his best.

III *The Winter Idyl*

Yet by almost unanimous consent, his longest poem is his best. *Snow-Bound: A Winter Idyl* has been described as "the greatest nineteenth-century poem of its type," a "composite of Yankee vignettes all mounted on one mat."[10] It has been compared, not always with excellent reason, to Robert Burns's "The Cotter's Saturday Night" and to Oliver Goldsmith's "The Deserted Village." Bliss Perry found it "notable, not so much for sensuous beauty or for any fresh ways of thought, as for its vividness, its fidelity to homely detail, its unerring feeling for the sentiment of the hearthside."[11] Edmund C. Stedman thought it superior to "Hermann and Dorothea," "Enoch Arden," or even "Evangeline"; for these poems, "memorable for beauty of another kind, leave the impression that each of their authors said, as Virgil must have, 'And now I will write an idyl.' Whittier found his idyl already pictured for him by the camera of his own heart."[12] The poet himself was more modest; he spoke of *Snow-Bound* as a collection of "Flemish pictures of old days" or, more simply, as "a picture of an old-fashioned farmer's fireside in winter—and if it were not mine," he added with as much whimsicality as guile, "I should call it pretty good."[13]

Most of these statements about *Snow-Bound* are probably true. The poem is a sublimation of the subjective, written with lyrical intensity in tender memory, as Whittier stated in its dedication, of the household which it describes. He had first thought of dedicating it to his brother, the only other surviving member of the Whittier family and also, except for the poet, the only member of the family not seen in the poem sitting about the family fire. He and his brother were the anonymous boys of *Snow-Bound* who watched enchanted as the storm swept through the farmyard, who dug a tunnel through the snow toward the barn, who listened—unseen to the reader—by the fire, and who in bed that night dreamed summer dreams. They alone of all the family later went out into the world. But more than this, *Snow-Bound* was written in 1865, soon after the death not only of Whittier's sister but of their mother; and, in the truest sense, the poem was a memorial to them and to the quiet happiness which their presence and that of other members of the family who were now gone had once brought.

The theme of *Snow-Bound* turns, as John Pickard has explained, "on the nostalgic recall of the love and protection which the Whittier family once gave the poet, emphasizing the powerful sense of present loss and hope for spiritual comfort. These emotions are primarily developed by a series of contrasts: of fire and snow, past and present, people and elements—which combine to form the larger theme of love and immortality struggling against pain and death." He suggests that a touchstone for interpreting the poem is the symbolic development of the wood fire, the physical comforts derived from its brightness and warmth compared to the emotional and spiritual warmth of family love.[14]

These things are in *Snow-Bound,* and they are woven together securely by the familiar unities of time, place, and mood; but it is not a static poem. Time moves steadily on—that is another of the things which the poem is about. After a night and a day of steady snowfall, the family sat snug beside its fire—"Shut from all the world without"—for an evening of companionship and story; the next morning, members of the family were wakened by the shout of teamsters clearing the highway; but it is a week before they have full contact with the world again. Within this simple pattern much is packed, just as Thoreau crammed into the cycle of a single year the experience of two years' residence beside Walden Pond. The remembered evening by the fire is filled with more tales than could possibly be told between sundown and a farm-boy's bedtime. Memories of many years are distilled to produce an essence more purely characteristic than any single evening could have been. Because it is thus compacted of a lifetime of feeling focused upon a single experience and what led up to it and what followed, *Snow-Bound* develops naturally through a pattern in which chronology and theme are intricately interwoven. Only when Whittier indulges himself by speaking, not in reminiscence, but of present thoughts, is the pattern broken. But even these personal interludes become part of an integral whole.

Depth of feeling and finely etched vignettes of people and place had characterized many of Whittier's earlier poems. Occasionally, as in "Skipper Ireson's Ride" and "Telling the Bees," these qualities had found coherence within patterns which have insured preservation to these poems—not because of the single excellence of any part, but through their wholeness as constructed entities. *Snow-Bound,* whether Whittier planned it so or not, is expertly patterned. It begins with a prelude made up of two quotations with which the poem is prefaced. The body of the poem is divided into three sections, each of which in turn is divided into parts. Each section is separated from the other by an interlude; and the whole is ended with a postlude which picks up, develops, and extends the theme suggested by the prelude at the beginning. The first section presents a mood of isolation; the second, of love and companionship; and the third, one created by the inevitable impingement of the world upon the quiet of wintry, rural solitude.

The introductory quotations set forth what seems at the beginning to have been considered its theme: the first from Agrippa's *Occult Philosophy* testifies to the superior power of light over darkness, even in the instance of "our common wood-fire" which, no less than the divine light of the sun, can drive away dark spirits; the second from Emerson's poem "The Snow Storm" speaks of housemates sitting about a radiant fireplace in a "tumultuous privacy of storm." Then the first

section of the poem, lines 1-178, is introduced by thirty lines
which describe the advent of the storm, the dark, circled sun,
the steady east wind, and the hurry of the farm household
in preparation for the coming of the snow. With line 31 comes
"the whirl-dance of the blinding storm" which, as darkness
fell quickly, piled white drifts against the window-frame; and
for the next one hundred and twenty-four lines the storm is
described: the marvelous shapes the snow took as it piled
on corn-crib, well-curb, or garden wall; the activities of the
family in digging a path to the barn and caring for livestock
there; the preparation of the evening fire, described in ex-
plicit detail:

> We piled with care our nightly stack
> Of wood against the chimney back—
> The oaken log, green, huge, and thick,
> And on its top the stout back-stick;
> The knotty forestick laid apart
> And filled between with curious art
> The ragged brush.

Outside the house, the whiteness of the snow, like the
whiteness of Melville's whale or the encompassing whiteness
which engulfs the climax of Poe's *Narrative of Arthur Gordon
Pym,* is awesome and large with implications better felt
than understood. All through this storm section the prevailing
tone, beyond that of muted wonder at the strange beauty
and fearsome menace of wind and snow and sleet, is of
isolation:

> Beyond the circle of our hearth
> No welcome sound of toil or mirth
> Unbound the spell, and testified
> Of human life and thought inside.

Yet the section ends with thirty-four lines of quiet exhilaration,
the family about the fire with house-dog and cat beside them,
with cider simmering on the hearth and apples sputtering in
a row. As so often in Hawthorne's tales, the cavernous hearth
can be thought of as a symbol of the human heart which,

when warmed by fires of love, is protected from all else besides:

> Blow high, blow low, not all its snow
> Could quench our hearth-fire's ruddy glow.

The second, longest, and central portion of the poem, lines 212-613, is separated from the first by an interlude of thirty-three lines in which Whittier comments on time and change; he recalls that his own hair now is as grey as his father's was on that winter evening long ago—

> How strange it seems, with so much gone
> Of life and love, to still live on!

Any life beyond this seemed no certainty, "yet love will dream, and Faith will trust" that somewhere, somehow, loved ones would meet again. Whittier pitied those

> Who hath not learned, in hours of faith,
>   The truth to flesh and sense unknown,
> That Life is ever lord of Death,
>   And Love can never lose its own!

Then for more than four hundred lines the evening by the fire is recalled, the yarns which were spun, the puzzles and riddles proposed, the schoolwork stammered through. The father's tales are remembered—of trapper's hut and Indian camp; of Norman village dances, fishing and clambakes; and of witchcraft—and then the mother's tales are recalled. Neither is described as a person except through the stories they told; but the bachelor uncle—innocent of books, simple, guileless, childlike—and the maiden aunt, the sweetest woman ever withheld from marriage by a perverse fate, are described in more detail; and so is the elder sister, impulsive, earnest, but ultimately unhappy. The younger sister, recently dead, said nothing; she only sat quietly with large, sweet, asking eyes. At the thought of her Whittier breaks into a thirty-eight line elegiac interlude, lines 400-437, which concludes the first part of the second section. Though isolated within by cold and snow, the family is firmly bound and protected by bonds of love.

The theme of the second part of the second section, lines 438-589, moves from recollection of family love to memory of widened horizons brought to the family group by the companionship of visitors from the world outside. The stories told about the fire in the first part had been of native experience or of local legend. In the second part, the schoolmaster brings lore from books; and the woman visitor brings an aura of tempestuous romance from a world quite beyond that known to any of the family. All of the best of life is there, centered about the homestead hearth. Isolated but compact, the universe was what they made it, these people by the blazing wood-fire, as their minds ranged in reminiscence over what they knew or had seen. Among the best of Whittier's character sketches, worthy of a place beside the portraits of ladies later done by Edwin Arlington Robinson, T. S. Eliot, and Ezra Pound, is that of Harriet Livermore, the eccentric and high-minded adventurer, battered by rebuffs in her attempts at reform:

> A woman tropical, intense
> In thought and act, in soul and sense,
> She blended in a like degree
> The vixen and the devotee,
> Revealing with each freak or feint
> The temper of Petruchio's Kate,
> The raptures of Sienna's saint.
> Her tapering hand and rounded wrist
> Had facile power to form a fist;
> The warm, dark languish of her eyes
> Was never safe from wrath's surprise.
> Brows saintly calm and lips devout
> Knew every change of scowl and pout;
> And the sweet voice had notes more high
> And shrill in social battle-cry.

The second section ends when at bedtime, nine o'clock, the uncle covered the fire with ashes—an action perhaps too undisguisedly symbolic—and the mother offered a brief prayer of gratitude "For food and shelter, warmth and health, And love's contentment." A brief interlude, lines 614-628, then introduces the third section, as the brothers lay abed listening to the wind roaring about the gables, loosening clapboards, sometimes beating with such force against the house that "our very bedsteads rock." But the peace of sleep came finally to them, so like the peace of death which was to take away every other member of the family. Whittier seldom wrote with more delicate suggestion:

> But sleep stole on, as sleep will do
> When hearts are light and life is new;
> Faint and more faint the murmurs grew,
> Till in the summer-land of dreams
> They softened to the sound of streams,
> Low stir of leaves, and dip of oars,
> And lapsing waves on quiet shores.

The third section, lines 629-714, opens with the coming of a second morning and the arrival of teamsters clearing the highway of snow. It was a community project, each farmer in turn lending his oxen and his labor to the task. Then came the village doctor on his sleigh, requiring neighborly assistance in the care of the sick. Work and duty call members of the family from the quiet comfort of their fireside. Finally, a week later, the local newspaper arrived; and the world was suddenly with them again—and all its practicality in measuring the depth, not the awesome beauty, of the snow; with its cold, pragmatic record of marriage, death, or imprisonment; with its quest and celebration of profit. The pulse of life about them seemed now to melt the "chill embargo of the snow," which had not really been chill at all; for it had provided the warmth of love and companionship. A careless reading can overlook the ironic ambiguity of the lines with which Whittier ends the section:

> Wide swing again our ice-locked door,
> And all the world was ours once more!

In conclusion, lines 715-759, the poet speaks in his present, lonely voice of that "spectral past" when the brightness of

[

a wood-fire drove away black spirits, when beside a radiant hearth happiness was found in spite of the tumult of the storm. *Snow-Bound* becomes then a parable of the life of any man, drawn by duty from the comfort of home ties; it becomes particularly a parable of Whittier's life, containing within it all for which he most had cared—a treasure chest crammed full of the people and the place, the kinds of legends of the past, and the lore of country life which formed the core of his existence. The fireside represented the kind of "insular Tahiti" of which Melville had spoken fifteen years earlier—a place of peaceful contentment to which, once having left it, no man could, nor indeed should, return. Here in comfort Whittier might have stayed, except that

> Importunate hours that hours succeed
> Each clamorous with its own sharp need,
>   And duty keeping pace with all.
> Shut down and clasp the heavy lids;
> I hear again the voice that bids
> The dreamer leave his dream midway
> For larger hopes and graver fears:
> Life threatens in these later years,
> The century's aloe flowers today!

This summons is not something which Whittier had not said before or would not say again. What distinguishes its statement in *Snow-Bound* beyond its statement almost anywhere else is that, though the words are not greatly better nor the feeling more intense than at other times, here it is firmly secured within a form which holds it firm as more than statement. What poetry has to say is not said alone by words which, as T. S. Eliot has explained,

> Crack and sometimes break under the burden,
> Under the tension, slip, slide, perish,
> Decay with imprecision. . . .

Only by the form—the pattern into which they are placed so that they play one upon another to suggest meanings beyond what is said—do they blend to become a poem. For this reason *Snow-Bound* becomes more than another exercise in nostalgic memory or a call for resolution in meeting the demands of duty; it shimmers with other suggestions. The past is good and beautiful and warm, like the wood-fire's blaze; and, in quiet moments, the benediction of memory is solace and joy; but life greatens when the present calls. In the last line quoted above, Whittier uses a favorite image of the century plant to say what Goethe said at the close of *Wilhelm Meister*, that America is here and now—and what T. S. Eliot meant when he said in "Burnt Norton"

> What might have been and what has been
> Point to one end, which is always present.

This comparison is not to imply that Whittier was a poet like T. S. Eliot or anyone else, or that he was a better or worse poet. What can be said is that occasionally he was a poet, and that his personal goodness and piety and gentleness contributed to and shine through that poetry. By themselves these qualities, whatever their excellence otherwise, can make a literary man a bore. Because goodness is a recognizable and eternal thing, what he says has so often been said, that one's answer to it is often a shrug—or an eye cocked for brighter, less hackneyed diversion. When the message is subdued, however, to the demands of art with its formal requirement of a beginning, a middle, and an end; when, without obtrusive intervention of the artist, one part is linked to another through image and extension of theme; and when self and art and moral are merged to one as they do merge in *Snow-Bound* but in so few of Whittier's other writings— then the poem becomes an entity which, once read, remains.

IV   *The Highest Reward*

Whittier composed many more lines during the next quarter century, but most of them were about subjects of which he had written better before. In "The Tent on the Beach" and the prelude to "Among the Hills" he spoke again with simple directness of his poetic creed and his hopes for humanity. "The Pennsylvania Pilgrim," though tediously long and repetitious, thought Barrett Wendell,[15] rang as wondrously free as ever in description of nature. Sarah Orne Jewett admired the nostalgic charm of "The Homestead," especially the "line about the squirrel in the house."[16] Matthew Arnold is said to have considered "In Schooldays" as "one of the perfect poems that must live"; and Oliver Wendell Holmes wept on first reading it—"the most beautiful schoolboy poem," he said, "in the English language." Some months later, in the fall of 1878, Holmes wrote his old friend: "I thank God that He has given you the thoughts and feelings which sing themselves as naturally as the wood-thrush rings his silver bell— to steal your own exquisitely descriptive line. Who has preached the gospel of love to such a mighty congregation as you have preached it? Who has done so much to sweeten the soul of Calvinistic New England? You have your reward here in the affection with which all our people, who are capable of loving anybody, regard you. I trust you will find a still higher, in that world the harmony of which finds an echo in so many of your songs."[17]

Although most of the poems after *Snow-Bound* were echoes, many of them were also portents of kinds of poetry to be written by other New England men who were boys during these latter years when Whittier lived quietly in his village home. If in his vignettes of country life, Whittier's simple colloquialism and instinctive fidelity to local scene reveal him as a literary ancestor of Robert Frost, his portraits of people suggest him equally an ancestor of Edwin Arlington Robinson who in "Miniver Cheevy," "Luke Havergal," and "Richard Cory" sketched character with no less insight but with more expert strokes. Robinson was fifteen when Whittier in 1884 wrote "Abram Morrison" as part of his contribution toward support of a charitable fair in Amesbury. The boy in Maine might even then have struck out several of the stanzas in which the more loquacious, older poet recorded his memory of an idiosyncratic Irish Quaker whom he had known long ago; but he certainly would have enjoyed some of them:

> 'Midst the men and things which will
> Haunt an old man's memory still,
> Drollest, quaintest of them all,

With a boy's laugh I recall
   Good old Abram Morrison.

. . . .

Wandering down from Nutfield woods
With his household and its goods,
Never was it clearly told
How within our quiet fold
   Came to be a Morrison.

. . . .

Simple-hearted, boy o'ergrown,
With a humour quite his own,
Of our sober-stepping ways,
Speech and look and cautious phrase,
   Slow to learn was Morrison.

Much we loved his stories told
Of a country strange and old,
Where the fairies danced till dawn,
And the goblin Leprecaun
   Looked, we thought, like Morrison.

Or wild tales of feud and fight,
Witch and troll and second sight
Whispered still where Stornoway
Looks across the stormy bay,
   Once the home of Morrisons.

. . . .

On his well-worn theme intent,
Simple, child-like, innocent,
Heaven forgive the half-checked smile
Of our careless boyhood, while
   Listening to Friend Morrison.

. . . .

Gone forever with the queer
Characters of that old year!
Now the many are as one;
Broken is the mould that run
   Men like Abram Morrison.

And broken perhaps is the mold also which produced the boy who became the man who remembered him.

Of the more than five hundred poems which Whittier included in his collected edition, perhaps only a dozen can be counted as surely successful. The following twelve seem to me Whittier's best, poems which might be included without apology in any Selected Edition of his writings: *Snow-Bound*, "Skipper Ireson's Ride," "Telling the Bees," "Ichabod," "Proem," "Prelude" to "Among the Hills," "Massachusetts to Virginia," "Letter from a Missionary. . . ," "The Henchman," "Laus Deo," "The Fruit Gift," and "Monadnock from Wachusett." Another group contains excellent poetry, but in poems more impressive when quoted in part than when read entire: "Mabel Martyn," "Kathleen," "The Witch of Wenham," "The Double-Headed Snake of Newbury," "The Prophecy of Samuel Sewall," "The Tent on the Beach," "The Panorama," "The Brewing of Soma," "The Waiting," "The Cypress Tree of Ceylon," "A Summer Pilgrimage," "The Last Walk in Autumn," "The Homestead," "The Old Burying Ground," "Abraham Davenport," and "Abram Morrison." No selection from Whittier would be representative, however, without some among the following more sentimental favorites: "Maud Muller," "The Barefoot Boy," "In Schooldays," "Barbara Frietchie," "Official Piety," and "Our Countrymen in Chains."

George Arms, in presenting a "new view" of Whittier in *The Fields Were Green,* defends and reprints "Birchbrook Hill," "The Pennsylvania Pilgrim," "Ichabod," "Skipper Ireson's Ride," "Maud Muller," "Barbara Frietchie," and *Snow-Bound.* Walt Whitman's friend William Sloane Kennedy—having made an appreciative bow toward *Snow-Bound* and "Ichabod" —named as "Whittier's best ballads": "Telling the Bees," "Maud Muller," "Barbara Frietchie," "Skipper Ireson's Ride," "The Witch's Daughter," and "The Witch of Wenham." These only, he said, were "free from the disfigurement . . . of so many of Whittier's descriptive pieces; namely, the moral at the end."[18]

Hyatt Waggoner is more generous. "The following poems," he says, "seem to me to offer the best basis for a defense of Whittier's achievement as a poet. They are at any rate the ones I have had chiefly in mind in making the claim that a significant number of his poems are still rewarding to read. It seems to me that many of the least known are better than those most commonly anthologized." He lists them then in the order which Whittier gave them in his final arrangement: "Telling the Bees," "The Double-Headed Snake of Newbury," "Mabel Martyn," "The Prophecy of Samuel Sewall," "Among the Hills" (the whole poem, but especially the "Prelude"), "The Pennsylvania Pilgrim," "The Fruit Gift," "The Old Burying Ground," "Monadnock from Wachusett," "A Summer Pilgrimage," "Ichabod," "The Tent on the Beach," "Massachusetts to Virginia," "The Christian Slave," "Lines from the Portrait. . . ," "The Panorama," "On a Prayer-Book," "My Namesake," *Snow-Bound*, "Laus Deo," "Trust," "Trinitas," and "Our Master."[19]

In these listings, only *Snow-Bound* and "Ichabod" stand out as unanimous choices. Perhaps it is by these two that Whittier will finally be remembered, along with "Telling the Bees" and "Skipper Ireson's Ride," both of which have attracted enthusiastic admirers. Each reader must finally make his own choice, for critics are notoriously better at finding faults than in recognizing superiority. To select so few of his poems as excellent is not, however, to suggest that many others among his verses—phrases, lines, often whole stanzas—will not continue to appeal to the emotion or imagination of many readers. "This," he once said, "is, after all, the highest reward of a writer, to know that suffering and sad hearts have been made happier by his words." Whittier never made high claims for his verses. "I am not one of the master singers," he confessed, "and don't pose as one. By the grace of God I am only what I am, and don't wish to pose as more."[20]

A dozen poems—or even four—is a generous legacy from any poet. Few among his countrymen have contributed more. Whittier was wrong when once, in a moment of despondency, he wrote: "We shall perish and verily *our works will follow us*. The hearts which now know us and love us will also cease to beat, and with them our memories will die. The utilitarian of the twentieth century will not heed whether, in treading on our graves, he shakes the dust of prose or poetry from his feet."[21] For Whittier does live on, recognized both as a courageous and a gentle man and as a gifted minor poet whom his countrymen may well remember with gratitude and pride. His limits are plainly marked, and by none more honestly than by himself.

Few poets are more comfortable to be with, for Whittier seldom makes any demand on readers other than to ask them to recognize with him that God is good, that nature is radiant with beauty, and that love is man's single shield against meanness and despair. Neither subtle nor complicated, and rarely perplexed either by sophistication or compromise, he speaks often of matters so radically profound that they require simplest statement. Late in life he wrote of "A Summer Pilgrimage" which took him once again to New England mountains amid whose untroubled quiet man and nature seemed momentarily at peace: behind the veils which beauty wove, man and mountain, lake, stream, and wood stood "witness to the Eternal Good." What the poet saw or felt or heard was an imperfect representation:

> A holier beauty overbroods
> These fair and faint similitudes.

Only undisturbed, familiar, and quiet words might reach toward truths which every man knew, and not in vain would be the reaching, though it failed to find its goal, for

> not unblest is he who sees
> Shadows of God's realities
> And knows beyond this masquerade
> Of shape and color, light and shade,
> And dawn and set, and wax and wane,
> Eternal verities remain.

Whittier's honesty and gentleness, his humility, and his quick anger at injustice certify him a good man, serene in faith which no experience could corrupt. His own life, as Whitman might have said, was his best poem, and *Snow-Bound* caught much of its essence. The journeyman verses excoriating slavery are part of the history of his time, testimonies to the purity of his intentions. Except occasionally, as in "Telling the Bees" and "Skipper Ireson's Ride," his narrative gift was not great. What seems most satisfactorily to survive are his portraits of people and his sketches of New England countryside—the vignettes, the pastorals, the idyls, the genre pieces, evocative of scene and character and mood. Though outlines are sometimes blurred with sentiment, the central portions usually stand clear, with trees, mountains, flowers, and people distinctly drawn. When he thus looked at objects and found words to reveal them, then he was a poet.

The goodness was always there, a precious possession, underlying and directing everything he wrote, and sometimes intruding. Without it, Whittier would have been someone else, a lesser man. To find the proper words and their necessary order, the artist's task, required discipline of a kind which neither Whittier's temperament nor time consistently provided. The wonder is that, unrestrained by criticism and unchallenged by effective competition, he should so often have done so well. That even in a few poems he surmounted his obvious shortcomings seems a miracle, as if Whittier, a rhymster by trade, was a poet by accident. Because poetry derives both from miracle and discipline, the point need not be labored. Whittier's achievement, small but unmistakably genuine, presents sufficient proof that on more than one occasion he submitted to both.

Notes and References

Chapter One

1. Whittier spoke often of his childhood, in letters, essays, and in reminiscent verse. The quotations in the preceding paragraphs are from "The Fish I Didn't Catch," first printed in *The Little Pilgrim* in Philadelphia in 1843, and collected in the Riverside Edition of *The Writings of John Greenleaf Whittier* (Boston and New York, 1889), V, 320-25; see also "Schoolday Remembrances," *op. cit.*, VI, 316-17. For ordinary details of Whittier's life, I have drawn on Samuel T. Pickard, *Life and Letters of John Greenleaf Whittier* (Boston and New York, 1894).

2. "Yankee Gypsies," *Writings*, V, 334.

3. William Sloane Kennedy, *John Greenleaf Whittier: The Poet of Freedom* (New York, 1892), 41n.-42n. Burns, said Whittier, "was the first poet I read, and will be the last."

4. Francis Mary Pray, *A Study of Whittier's Apprenticeship As a Poet* (State College, Pennsylvania, 1930), p. 5, supposes that the "family library was limited to about thirty volumes, mostly of the pious type, so that the youthful Whittier's desire for stories was satisfied for the most part by accounts of martyrs in the cause of religion, by *Pilgrim's Progress,* or the narrative chapters of the Bible. Until he was fourteen years old the Bible and Burns's poems were about the only good poetic material Whittier ever encountered." See John A. Pollard, *John Greenleaf Whittier: Friend of Man* (Boston, 1949), pp. 589-92, for a listing of John Whittier's library.

5. *William Lloyd Garrison: The Story of His Life* (New York, 1884), I, 67; quoted in George Rice Carpenter, *John Greenleaf Whittier* (New York and Boston, 1903), pp. 39-40.

6. *Newburyport Free Press,* June 22, 1821.

7. Carpenter, *John Greenleaf Whittier,* p. 40.

8. *Essex Gazette,* May 17, 1828. "Our poetical correspondent, 'W,' is a young man belonging to the society of Friends in this town," said Thayer, "only 17 years of age, an Apprentice to a mechanical business [shoemaking], and has never enjoyed any other advantages of education than such as are afforded in our common schools. His effusions . . . indicate, we should say,

considering his disadvantages, a genius unparalleled among American poets."

9. *Essex Gazette*, January 24, 1828. A week later the *Boston Statesman*, January 21, 1828, spoke of Whittier's verses as "evidently put forth by a mind of more than ordinary strength," and of the young poet as "one whom we trust to hail among the foremost of our native bards."

10. Pickard, *Life*, I, 70.

11. *Ibid.*, I, 93-94.

12. *Ibid.*, I, 100.

13. *Ibid.*, I, 101.

14. *Ibid.*, I, 113.

15. Whitman Bennett, *Whittier: Bard of Freedom* (Chapel Hill, North Carolina, 1941), p. 70.

16. Pickard, *Life*, I, 101-2, 114.

Chapter Two

1. *New England Weekly Review*, June 29, 1929. See Thomas Franklin Currier, "Whittier and the *New England Weekly Review*," *New England Quarterly*, VI (September, 1933), 589-97.

2. See Edwin Harrison Cady and Harry Hayden Clark, *Whittier on Writers and Writing: The Uncollected Critical Writings of John Greenleaf Whittier* (Syracuse, 1950), p. 93.

3. *New England Weekly Review*, September 13, 1830.

4. See Kennedy, *John Greenleaf Whittier*, pp. 94, 96.

5. Whittier excluded the poem from his collected *Writings*. In response to an inquiry about it in 1884, he wrote: "The pamphlet described in thy note I am ashamed to own as mine. I had hoped it had died out of print and am rather sorry that old Moll has materialized herself." See *Bookman*, VIII (September, 1898), 42; quoted in Thomas Franklin Currier, *A Bibliography of John Greenleaf Whittier* (Cambridge, 1937), p. 20.

6. Pickard, *Life*, I, 393-94.

7. July 16, 1829.

8. Pickard, *Life*, I, 113-14, 116.

9. *Ibid.*, I, 121.

10. *Ibid.*, II, 505.

11. See, for example, Albert Mordell, *Quaker Militant: John Greenleaf Whittier* (Boston, 1933).

12. Whittier's antislavery writings in prose have not been completely collected from the files of various periodicals in which they appeared. Some are included in Volume VII of the River-

side Edition of the *Writings,* including *Justice and Expediency,* from which I have quoted at large. See especially, "What is Slavery?" and "Democracy and Slavery." Whitman Bennett in *Whittier: Bard of Freedom,* pp. 79-84, provides an excellent summary of *Justice and Expediency,* as does also Harry Hayden Clark, *John Greenleaf Whittier: Representative Selections* (New York, 1935). Howard R. Floan, *The South in Northern Eyes, 1831 to 1861* (Austin, Texas, 1958), gives a summary account of Whittier's attitudes toward slavery and of some of the sources of his information on the subject.

13. Pickard, *Life,* I, 187.

14. Currier, *Bibliography,* p. 30.

15. See *Ibid.,* pp. 32-33, for some details of the controversy over the pamphlet, which southern opponents claimed to have been written by "some peddling Yankee preacher," eager to create a scandal and make money from it.

16. See "The Bible and Slavery," *Writings,* VII, 96-99. Whittier was especially bitter against clergymen who apologized for slavery and who quoted from the Bible to support their position: "If the Bible does sanction the vilest wrong which man can inflict upon his fellow-man, if it does rivet the chains which humanity, left to itself, would otherwise cast off, then, in humanity's name, let it perish from the face of the earth" (*Ibid.,* p. 95). On the other hand, he habitually pictured Negroes as pious, God-fearing, Bible-loving people.

17. *Writings,* VII, 13.

18. Whittier once gave as his reasons for not marrying: "Circumstances—the care of an aged mother, the duty owed to a sister in delicate health for many years—must be my excuse for living the lonely life." (Pickard, *Life,* I, 276). Thomas Franklin Currier, "Whitman's Philadelphia Friends," *Bulletin of the Friends Historical Association,* XXVII (August, 1938), 58-72, and *Elizabeth Lloyd and the Whittiers: A Budget of Letters* (Cambridge, 1939), detail Whittier's personal relations during this period in the 1830's, showing him, though a busy man, fond of quiet society and the companionship of friends. His letters and those of his sister to the young Quaker poet, Elizabeth Lloyd, reveal the depths of their dedication to abolition and the warmth of their friendship. "It is not strange," says Currier (p. xi), "that such sympathetic and congenial young persons as Elizabeth and Greenleaf, aged twenty-seven and thirty-one respectively, should have been drawn irresistibly to each other, but a careful reading of the letters here presented and of other documents has not given any reason to believe that they had, at this period, any serious

thoughts of becoming engaged." After Miss Lloyd's marriage in 1853 and her husband's death three years later, she continued in infrequent but affectionate correspondence with the Whittiers. See also M. V. Denervaud, *Whittier's Unknown Romance* (Boston, 1922); Albert Mordell, "Whittier and Lucy Hopper," *New England Quarterly*, VII (January, 1934), 316-25; G. F. Shepard, "Letters of Lucy Larcom to the Whittiers," *New England Quarterly*, III (July, 1930), 501-18; and Samuel T. Pickard, "A Merry Woman's Letters to a Quiet Poet," *Ladies Home Journal*, XVII (December, 1899, January, 1900), 7-8, 9-10.

19. Pickard, *Life*, I, 218, 240-43.

20. *Ibid.*, I, 259.

Chapter Three

1. See "Letter to Samuel Sewall," *Writings*, VII, 87-92.

2. Currier, *Elizabeth Lloyd and the Whittiers*, pp. 17-18.

3. Almost all critics who have known Whittier and his writings well have treated him and his motives with sympathy and respect. Others who have glanced at him briefly have often been less sympathetic, particularly, it has seemed to me, in the classroom, where Whittier is sometimes dismissed with a witticism. Albert Mordell in *Quaker Militant*, though admiring Whittier for other things, does not seem always sympathetic in dealing with the poet's personal life. For an interpretation mildly Freudian, see Ludwig Lewisohn, *Expression in America* (New York, 1932). Paul Elmer More, "Whittier the Poet," *Shelborne Essays, Third Series* (New York, 1906), pp. 28-53, presents a more reasoned estimate. See also Bliss Perry, "Whittier for Today," *Atlantic Monthly*, C (December, 1907), 851-54, and H. H. Hurd, "Paradoxes in the Life and Poetry of John Greenleaf Whittier," *Poetry Review*, XVII (August, 1926), 261-67.

4. George Rice Carpenter, *John Greenleaf Whittier* (Boston and New York, 1903), p. 212.

5. Currier, *Bibliography*, p. 47.

6. "The City of a Day," *Writings*, V, 351.

7. *Ibid.*, pp. 353-54.

8. "The Lighting Up," *Writings*, V, 380.

9. "The First Day in Lowell," *Writings*, V, 373-74.

10. "Pawtucket Falls," *Writings*, V, 363-64.

11. Pickard, *Life*, I, 336.

12. Currier, *Bibliography*, p. 82.

13. Pickard, *Life,* II, 413, 425n., 436; Kennedy, *John Greenleaf Whittier,* pp. 134-35.
14. Pickard, *Life,* II, 502.
15. Bennett, *Whittier,* p. 267.
16. Pickard, *Life,* II, 469, 471.

Chapter Four

1. Pickard, *Life,* II, 481.
2. Currier, *Bibliography,* pp. 98-100; Pickard, *Life,* II, 407, 492-93.
3. Pickard, *Life,* II, 513.
4. *Ibid.,* II, 523-24.
5. *Ibid.,* II, 512.
6. *Ibid.,* II, 529.
7. *Ibid.,* II, 595.
8. J. C. Derby, *Fifty Years Among Authors, Books, and Publishers* (New York, 1884), p. 282.
9. Pickard, *Life,* II, 675.
10. *Ibid.,* II, 603.
11. *Ibid.,* II, 731-32.

Chapter Five

1. Pickard, *Life,* II, 692.
2. July 16, 1829; see Cady and Clark, *Whittier on Writers,* pp. 25-26.
3. Cady and Clark, *Whittier on Writers,* p. 26.
4. *New England Weekly Review,* August 9, 1830; see Cady and Clark, *Whittier on Writers,* pp. 46-47.
5. Whittier's early literary judgments are excellently summarized by Edwin Harrison Cady in the introduction to Cady and Clark, *Whittier on Writers,* pp. 2-14; see also John B. Pickard, "The Basis of Whittier's Critical Creed: The Beauty of the Commonplace and the Truth of Style," *Rice Institute Pamphlet,* XLVII (October, 1960), 34-47. Harry Hayden Clark, *Major American Poets* (New York, 1936), pp. 802-16, traces a three-fold maturing of the poet from romanticism through political liberalism to religious humanism. Clarence Arthur Brown, *The Achievement of American Criticism* (New York, 1954), pp. 169-71, places Whittier's critical views in historical perspective.
6. "Whittier the Poet," pp. 43-44.

7. Pickard, *Life,* II, 677.

8. *Ibid.,* II, 203.

9. Cady and Clark, *Whittier on Writers,* pp. 11-12. For a detailed analysis of Whittier's verse forms, see Gay Wilson Allen, *American Prosody* (New York, 1935); see also K. A. McEuen, "Whittier's Rhymes," *American Speech,* XX (February, 1945), 81-87.

10. "The Poetry of Heart and Home," *National Era,* September 9, 1847; see Cady and Clark, *Whittier on Writers,* p. 121.

11. "What I Had I Gave: Another Look at Whittier," *Essex Institute Historical Collections,* XVI (January, 1959), 32-40.

12. Kennedy, *John Greenleaf Whittier,* pp. 220-21.

13. "Patucket Falls," *Writings,* V, 361-62, 367; see also "The Beautiful," *ibid.,* 413-14, 416.

14. Pickard, *Life,* I, 213.

15. See John B. Pickard, "The Basis of Whittier's Critical Creed," pp. 34-48.

Chapter Six

1. "What I Had I Gave," *op. cit.,* pp. 38-39.

2. "What Is Slavery?" *Writings,* VII, 100-7.

3. Clark, *Major American Poets,* pp. 802-4, finds Whittier's ideas, as influenced by his allegiance to humanitarian philanthropy, his Quaker faith, his devotion to Puritan liberalism as represented by John Milton and Andrew Marvell, and the natural rights philosophies of the radical Thomas Paine and the conservative Edmund Burke, to have passed through three distinct stages: "[1] Up to 1833 he was chiefly interested as a fanciful romanticist and apostle of Scott-like localism [and Burns-like concern with common things and common people, and their superstitions], in the lurid, the strange, the sensational, or the dreamy; [2] from 1833 to about 1859 [when he began to contribute regularly and profitably to the *Atlantic Monthly*] he was chiefly interested as a political liberal in emancipation, sympathy, and social reform to be effected by outward means; and [3] from about 1859 to his death he transcended his earlier interests by including them in a more comprehensive philosophy, in religious humanism chiefly concerned with helping the individual to find spiritual peace through self-conquest, through reliance on the fact that man is endowed with the power of bringing his conduct, through free will and self-discipline, into fruitful harmony with Divine Law revealed to him through the Interior

Light of aspiration shining through the dark impulses of natural man." Henry W. Wells, *The American Way of Poetry* (New York, 1949), p. 45, discovers Whittier "one-third democrat, one-third sheer dullness, and one-third genuine poet . . . one of the genuine products of the folk culture of Protestant New England." H. H. Hurd, "Paradoxes in the Life and Poetry of John Greenleaf Whittier," p. 264, finds him "a man of limited culture" who violated the conventions of versification; Van Wyck Brooks, *The Flowering of New England, 1815-1865* (New York, 1936), pp. 198-200, is also unsympathetic.

4. "Whittier's ICHABOD, 33-36," *Explicator*, XVIII (April, 1960), item 38. Mr. Maddox further explains that the "scriptural reference gives an effective double sense to 'walk backward' and especially to 'pay the reverence of old days,' which thus becomes an injunction: (1) to cherish the thought of Webster as he was in his former and better days, and (2) to practice, even under circumstances which might excuse an opposite course, the decent piety evinced by Shem and Japheth and enjoined in such old-time precepts as appear in *Exodus*, XX, 12, and *Leviticus*, XVIII, 6."

5. Bennett, *Whittier*, pp. 270-74.

Chapter Seven

1. *The Fields Were Green: A New View of Bryant, Whittier, Holmes, Lowell, and Longfellow* (Stanford, California, [1953]), pp. 38-39.

2. "Whittier's Ballads: The Maturing of an Artist," *Essex Institute Historical Collections*, XCVI (January, 1960), 56-72; see also Mr. Pickard's *The Artistry of Whittier*, unpublished University of Wisconsin doctoral dissertation, 1954.

3. "Poetry in America: A New Consideration of Whittier's Poetry," *New England Quarterly*, VII (June, 1934), 259.

Chapter Eight

1. *The Spirit of American Literature* (New York, 1913), p. 121.

2. Quoted in Edmund Clarence Stedman, *The Poets of America* (Boston and New York, 1885), p. 604.

3. "Poetry in America," *op. cit.*, p. 273.

4. *Expression in America*, p. 127.

5. Pickard, *Life*, II, 364.

6. *Ibid.*, II, 593.

7. *The Fields Were Green*, p. 6.

8. "Whittier's Ballads," *op. cit.*, p. 68.

9. Pickard, *Life*, II, 428, 453.

10. John A. Pollard, *John Greenleaf Whittier: Friend to Man* (Boston, 1949), p. 265.

11. *John Greenleaf Whittier: A Sketch of His Life* (Boston, 1907), p. 28.

12. *Poets of America*, p. 117.

13. Pickard, *Life*, II, 497-98.

14. "Imagistic and Structural Unity in 'Snow-Bound,' " *College English*, XXI (March, 1960), 34-50. Mr. Pickard discovers a structure in *Snow-Bound* somewhat simpler than the one which I outline; his treatment of the whole poem, however, is the most expert and sympathetic which I have seen.

15. "John Greenleaf Whittier," *Stelligeri and Other Essays Concerning America* (New York, 1893), pp. 166-67.

16. Quoted in Pickard, *Life*, II, 718-19. Whittier admired Miss Jewett's writings also. In 1879 he wrote to her: "I have read 'Deephaven' over half a dozen times, and always with gratitude to thee for such a book—so simple, pure, and so true to nature. And 'Old Friends and New' I shall certainly read as often. When tired and worried I resort to thy books and find rest and refreshing. I recommend them to everybody, and everybody likes them. There is no dissenting opinion; and already thousands whom thee have never seen love the author as well as her books" (Pickard, *Life*, II, 654).

17. Pickard, *Life*, II, 644.

18. *John Greenleaf Whittier*, p. 221.

19. "What I Had I Gave," *op. cit.*, p. 40n.

20. Quoted in Jay B. Hubbell, *American Life in Literature* (New York, 1949), I, 565.

21. Quoted in Scott, "Poetry in America," *op. cit.*, p. 274-75.

Selected Bibliography

WHITTIER'S WORKS

The most complete edition of Whittier's writings, edited by Horace E. Scudder, with Whittier's assistance, is *The Writings of John Greenleaf Whittier* (Boston and New York: Houghton Mifflin Company, 1888-89), 7 vols., reissued, 1904; see Eleanor M. Tilton, "Making Whittier Definitive," *New England Quarterly*, XII (June, 1939), 281-84. This edition forms the basis of Scudder's one-volume Cambridge Edition, *The Complete Poems of John Greenleaf Whittier* (Boston and New York: Houghton Mifflin Company, 1894). An excellently edited text is Harry Hayden Clark's *John Greenleaf Whittier: Representative Selections, with Introduction, Bibliography, and Notes* (New York: American Book Company, 1935).

Bibliographically, Whittier is exhaustively explained in Thomas Franklin Currier, *A Bibliography of John Greenleaf Whittier* (Cambridge: Harvard University Press, 1937). For later periodical writings concerning him, see Lewis Leary, ed., *Articles on American Literature, 1900-1950* (Durham, North Carolina: Duke University Press, 1954), pp. 316-19.

SECONDARY SOURCES

The following selective list includes biographical and critical writings useful to the student of Whittier.

ALLEN, GAY WILSON. *American Prosody*. New York: American Book Company, 1935. An examination of Whittier's versification, which discovers him "almost never spontaneously lyrical, [nor] overflowing the bounds of rules because the poet feels more emotion than he can express by 'the tricks of art.'"

ARMS, GEORGE. *The Fields Were Green: A New View of Bryant, Whittier, Holmes, Lowell, and Longfellow, with a Selection of Their Poems*. Stanford, California: Stanford University Press (1953). A mature, fresh estimation of the "schoolroom poets," which finds Whittier not only "an important man in history and a noble man in his own right," but also "sometimes a poet by a most exacting scale."

Selected Bibliography

BENNETT, WHITMAN. *Whittier*: *Bard of Freedom*. Chapel Hill: University of North Carolina Press, 1941. An enthusiastic defense of Whittier, emphasizing his early life and his anti-slavery activities.

BOYNTON, H. W. "John Greenleaf Whittier, an Appreciation," *Putnam's Magazine*, III (December, 1907), 274-80. A sensible and moderate estimate which places the poet against the background of his times.

CADY, EDWIN HARRISON, and HARRY HAYDEN CLARK. *Whittier on Writers and Writing*: *The Uncollected Critical Writings of John Greenleaf Whittier*. Syracuse: Syracuse University Press, 1950. The best introduction to Whittier's early literary attitudes, and the most complete collection of his early critical writing.

CARPENTER, GEORGE RICE. *John Greenleaf Whittier*. Boston and New York: Houghton Mifflin Company, 1903. A pleasantly written and judicious contribution to the American Men of Letters Series; based on information drawn almost entirely from Pickard, *Life* (see below), but enlivened with independent, sensitive critical remarks.

CHRISTY, ARTHUR. "The Orientalism of Whittier," *American Literature*, V (November, 1933), 247-57. Except for his knowledge of the Bible, Whittier's information on the literature of the East came to him at second hand.

CURRIER, THOMAS FRANKLIN. *Elizabeth Lloyd and the Whittiers*: *A Budget of Letters*. Cambridge: Harvard University Press, 1939. The correspondence here brought together by the most prominent Whittier scholar of the early twentieth century presents fair evidence that Whittier, though a friendly man and sociable, did not often worry about being a bachelor.

————. "Whittier and the *New England Weekly Review*," *New England Quarterly*, VI (September, 1938), 589-97. The most complete examination of Whittier's activities as an editor in Hartford.

————. "Whittier's Philadelphia Friends," *Bulletin of the Friends Historical Association*, XXVII (August, 1938), 58-72. Although busy with propaganda and editorial duties in Philadelphia in the late 1830's, Whittier did find time for social and religious meetings with fellow Quakers, some of whom did not approve of his strenuous, un-Quakerlike activities in reform.

FLOAN, HOWARD R. *The South in Northern Eyes, 1831-1861*. Austin: University of Texas Press, 1955. A helpful but not exhaustive survey of Whittier's pre-Civil War attitudes toward the South.

FOERSTER, NORMAN. *Nature in American Literature*. New York: The Macmillan Company, 1923. A classic critical study of Whittier's attitudes toward landscape and man: "Much as he loved Nature . . . Whittier was a religious poet," and Christian character was more important to him than art.

HAWKINS, CHAUNCEY J. *The Mind of Whittier: A Study of Whittier's Fundamental Ideas*. New York: Thomas J. Hawkins, 1904. Based chiefly on his religious thought.

JONES, RUFUS M. "Whittier's Fundamental Religious Faith," *Byways of Quaker History*, ed., HOWARD H. BRINTON. Wallingford, Pennsylvania, 1944. Whittier's Quakerism is explained and defended by a latter-day spokesman for the Friends.

KENNEDY, WILLIAM SLOANE. *John Greenleaf Whittier: The Poet of Freedom*. New York: Funk and Wagnalls Company, 1892. Emphasizes the virtues of the man more highly than those of the poet: "in more than one third of his poems freedom is either the main theme or is alluded to in passing."

MCEUEN, KATHRYN ANDERSON. "Whittier's Rhymes," *American Speech*, XX (February, 1945), 81-87. Whittier's rhyming is not so careless as sometimes stated: his occasional derelictions can be explained by the strong emotion behind many of his occasional pieces, his meager formal education, and his adherence to regional pronunciation.

MORDELL, ALBERT. *Quaker Militant: John Greenleaf Whittier*. Boston: Houghton Mifflin Company, 1933. A distractingly interesting biographical study which is distorted by the author's undocumented certainty that Whittier was a philanderer and a "male coquette"; though as one-sided as Whittier himself in attitudes toward slavery, the author presents a lively and convincing account of the poet's activities as editor and propagandist.

PERRY, BLISS. *John Greenleaf Whittier: A Sketch of His Life*. Boston and New York: Houghton Mifflin Company, 1907. Judiciously appreciative, perhaps the best short introduction to Whittier's writings.

PICKARD, JOHN B. "The Basis of Whittier's Critical Creed: The Beauty of the Commonplace and the Truth of Style," *Rice Institute Pamphlet*, XLVII (October, 1960), 34-50. The most complete statement of Whittier's literary attitudes: "The best of Whittier's genre pieces and his ballads illustrate the essential truth . . . that underneath the most commonplace objects lay beauty, rich treasures of life's tragedy and comedy. His regional works reveal the inner love of a man for the environment that molded him, the tradition that inspired him, and the people that loved him."

—————. "Imagistic and Structural Unity in 'Snow-Bound,'" *College English*, XXI (March, 1960), 338-42. A reading of Whittier's poem which demonstrates how structure adds richness to meaning.

—————. "Whittier's Ballads: The Maturing of an Artist," *Essex Institute Historical Collections*, XCVI (January, 1960), 56-73. When he returned to home scenes and local themes, Whittier fulfilled much of the promise which he had shown as a youth.

PICKARD, SAMUEL T. *Life and Letters of John Greenleaf Whittier*. Boston and New York: Houghton Mifflin Company, 1894. The standard, indispensable biography, drawn on by almost all succeeding writers.

POLLARD, JOHN A. *John Greenleaf Whittier: Friend to Man*. Boston: Houghton Mifflin Company, 1949. The most complete and dependable modern biography, well documented and judicious; a necessary supplement to Pickard's *Life*.

POWELL, DESMOND. "Whittier," *American Literature*, IX (November, 1937), 335-42. A sensitive and revealing critical study which identifies Whittier as a poet worthy of study and respect.

PRAY, FRANCES MARY. *A Study of Whittier's Apprenticeship As a Poet*. State College: Pennsylvania State College Press, 1930. Dealing with poems written between 1825 and 1835 not included in the collected *Writings*.

QUINN, DOROTHY M. and WILLIAM R. "Barbara Frietschie," *Maryland Historical Magazine*, XXXVII (September, December, 1942), 227-54, 401-3. An identification of the heroine of Whittier's poem, and an examination of its truth to history: Mrs. Frietschie [sic] was there all right, but was sick in bed at the time.

SCOTT, WINFIELD TOWNLEY. "Poetry in America: A New Consideration of Whittier's Poetry," *New England Quarterly*, VII (June, 1934), 258-75. A dignified, appreciative defense: "In his *Songs of Labor*, he antedated Whitman's celebration of the workingman by four years. In looking for American legends, he anticipated Hawthorne. . . . He created a handful of enduring poems."

STEVENS, J. S. *Whittier's Use of the Bible*. Orono: University of Maine Studies, 1930. A useful but incomplete listing of Whittier's scriptural allusions.

WAGGONER, HYATT H. "What I Had I Gave: Another Look at Whittier," *Essex Institute Historical Collections*, XVI (January, 1959), 32-40. An acute but sympathetic critical account: "Not just American life but American poetry too is richer because he lived and wrote."

Index

Index

Index